PRO-ACTIVE MANAGEMENT

PRO-ACTIVE MANAGEMENT

How to Improve Your Management Performance

Neil M. Glass

cartoons by Morten Schmidt

CASSELL

East Brunswick, New Jersey

Cassell Educational Limited
Villiers House, 41/47 Strand, London WC2N 5JE, England
Published in the United States of America by **Nichols Publishing**,
11 Harts Lane, East Brunswick, NJ 08816

© Neil M. Glass 1991

First published 1991

British Library Cataloguing in Publication Data
Glass, Neil M.
    Pro-active management
    1. Management
    I. Title
    658

ISBN 0-304-33008-6 (hardback)
        0-304-33006-X (paperback)

Library of Congress Cataloging-in-Publication Data
Glass, Neil M.
    Pro-active management : how to improve your management performance / Neil M. Glass.
        p.   cm.
    ISBN 0-89397-410-2 (p)
    1. Management.   I. Title.
    HD31.G5379 1991
    658—dc20   90-27156
                                                                                      CIP

Typeset by Saxon Printing Ltd, Derby.
Printed and bound in Great Britain by
Dotesios Ltd, Wiltshire.

Contents

Introduction   *vii*

Managing people   *1*

1   Motivation   *2*
2   The manager's role   *6*
3   Management style   *10*
4   Increasing employee involvement   *15*
5   Negotiation   *19*
6   Transactional Analysis   *23*

Groups and meetings   *27*

7   Group formation   *28*
8   Group behaviour and roles   *31*
9   Negative aspects of groups   *35*
10   Effective meetings   *39*

The nature of organizations   *43*

11   Organization structure   *44*
12   Changing organization structure   *48*
13   Organizational culture   *52*
14   Organizations as political systems   *56*
15   Power in organizations   *59*

Managing change   *63*

16   Change and resistance   *64*
17   Sensing the problem   *68*
18   Starting the change process   *70*
19   Managing the change process   *74*
20   Common responses to the need for change   *78*

Strategy   *83*

21   SWOT analysis   *84*
22   Portfolio analysis – introduction   *88*
23   Portfolio analysis – alternative views   *93*
24   Industry structure analysis   *98*
25   Supply chain analysis   *102*

26   A definition of strategy   *107*
27   Managing turnaround   *113*

Marketing   *119*

28   The marketing concept   *120*
29   Differential advantage   *124*
30   Developing a marketing strategy   *127*
31   Consumer behaviour   *132*
32   Setting prices   *136*
33   Marketing and the product life cycle   *140*
34   Industrial marketing   *144*
35   Marketing services   *147*
36   Writing a marketing plan   *150*

Creative problem-solving   *153*

37   Creative thinking   *154*
38   Brainstorming   *158*
39   Problem-solving   *162*
40   Mind-mapping   *166*
41   Quality circles   *170*
42   Other creative-thinking techniques   *174*

Lessons from Japan   *177*

43   Japan and the West   *178*
44   'Market share' versus 'financial' strategy   *182*
45   Maximize customer satisfaction   *186*
46   The importance of quality   *189*
47   Just-in-time production   *193*
48   Getting the best from people   *197*
49   Role of the trade unions   *202*

50   Fashions, fads and quick fixes   *205*

References   *209*
Index   *211*

Introduction

What are group think, satisficing, mind-mapping, portfolio analysis, matrix structures, power cultures, gate-keepers, force field analysis, emergent behaviour, differentiation and SWOTs? And do we even need to know, anyway?

We are living in a world where packaging is increasingly more important than content and where politicians can be elected on the basis of a few seconds of carefully-chosen 'sound-bite'. This 'sound-bite' culture has affected most aspects of our lives. In business books, for example, new gurus tell us that we will all suddenly become effective and successful by following six or seven simple rules or by dedicating one minute a day to managing. Knowledge is apparently no longer important. Good management can be picked up from best-selling books. Hard work and study are things of the past.

Unfortunately, this book takes a different approach. We believe that knowledge has an important part to play in any manager's development. Good management must be a combination of ability, experience and knowledge - it is our aim to try and provide a significant part of that knowledge in an easily accessible form. In some business books, it can be difficult to separate the real content from the mass of preamble, examples, explanations and general filling. We have tried to reduce inessential material to a minimum, so that we can provide as much useful information as possible.

Pro-Active Management is structured with ease of use in mind. It is divided into eight main parts covering topics ranging from the 'people' aspects of management – Managing People, Groups and Meetings, the Nature of Organizations, Managing Change – to more technical areas such as Strategy and Marketing. A key section deals with Creative Problem-Solving, because this will be increasingly important as organizations and their environments become more complex. The book ends with lessons from Japan, as it is clear that Japan will continue to provide a model of good management practice for us in the West. The eight parts are further split into 50 chapters, so the book can either be read through, taken in short self-contained sections or else used as a reference.

If there is a theme or message in this book, then it is that we in the West have still not fully understood how to get the best from the people we work with. Our organizations tend to be highly structured with orders coming down, but little communication going up. We often act as if managers are hired from the shoulders up and workers from the shoulders down. When we do encourage employee participation in decision-making, it tends to be just 'lifeboat democracy' – a last-ditch effort, when all else has failed. For us, managers have careers while workers have jobs – managers are educated while workers are trained. And behind all this we have developed financial systems where short-term gain is more important than long-term growth, and where those who make the money are not those who create the wealth.

Until we start to address these issues, we will continue to be surprised as our competitors go from strength to strength at our expense.

Throughout the book the word 'he' is used as a general term for convenience and to avoid repeating 'he or she', though on all occasions the feminine pronoun would be equally applicable.

MANAGING PEOPLE

1 Motivation

2 The manager's role

3 Management style

4 Increasing employee involvement

5 Negotiation

6 Transactional Analysis

1
Motivation

Most of us believe we are expert judges of human behaviour – both of ourselves and of other people. This is strange for two reasons. Firstly, because unless we have studied psychology, our education is unlikely to have included any formal teaching of the theory of human personality and motivation. Secondly, because the level of conflict, open or suppressed, in many organizations suggests we are not as successful as we would like to believe, in understanding either ourselves or others. It may, therefore, be helpful to learn and apply some of the more practical models of human behaviour which have been developed.

Maslow's Hierarchy of Needs

There are many theories of behaviour to choose from, but one of the most useful general approaches to motivation was developed by Professor Abraham Maslow. Maslow identified five types of need which he rated on an ascending scale, as in the figure.

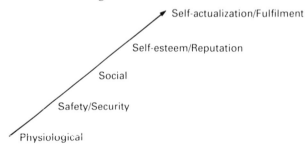

Figure 1

The main characteristics of each need were:

Physiological needs such as hunger, thirst, sex and shelter are basic to ensuring survival.

Safety/Security needs can range from protection against threats from the environment and others to our desire for stability, order and predictability in our lives and work.

Social needs include our need to belong to a group, to gain colleagues' acceptance and to give and receive love and affection.

Self-esteem/Reputation refers to our need to build up our personal worth through reputation, recognition, respect and self-confidence based on our achievements.

Self-actualization/Fulfilment concerns our need to develop to our full potential, to be creative, to feel we are contributing something worthwhile.

His theory was that only when each lower need was satisfied does the next, higher need become important to us. If we are hungry we will not worry about our social position. If we are anxious about our job security, we will not be concerned over how satisfying the actual work is. But the less a need is satisfied the more important it becomes to us.

The relevance of this theory to managers is that it can help them understand how to get the best from their people. Firstly, it highlights the limited power of money to achieve improved performance. Once staff are earning what they believe to be reasonable pay, they will start to look for other things like job interest and satisfaction, social respect and self-development. Too often managers fail to identify this change in their people's priorities. They try to deal with performance by inventing ever more complex, expensive and unwieldy bonus schemes instead of addressing the real issues, which might be boredom, desire for more responsibility, or dissatisfaction with work conditions.

We, in the West, are good at expressing our lower-order needs – for food, sex, security – but very bad at articulating the higher needs. If we are unhappy in our jobs, we tend to become negative to our employer and only do what we think is necessary to maintain our position. Or else we may withdraw into ourselves and again our performance drops. But most commonly, when we cannot get what we want from a job, we ask for more of what we believe we can get. Too often, workers who are dissatisfied with conditions, management's attitudes, their company's overall performance or their job structures will react by demanding more money. A process of conflict or bargaining then follows. But a satisfactory solution is never found, as money was not the real issue in the first place. Seldom, if ever, does a trade union ask for more responsibility for members, or improved, more interesting jobs. Yet too frequently these are precisely the causes of dissatisfaction which misleadingly and destructively find expression in demands for more pay.

A sobering comment on the nature of most organizations and the ability of managers to get the best from their staff, is that one standard management text suggests that 'very few people will ever satisfy their self-actualization needs at work'.

Maslow's hierarchy of needs has been accused of being too simple and only being relevant to Western (in particular, American) society. However, it does provide a useful way for managers, workers and unions to clarify what people's underlying aspirations might be, and by responding to them they can avoid unnecessary dissatisfaction or conflict.

While the hierarchy of needs gives a general picture of group and individual motivation, it is not detailed enough to give a workable way of guiding how we should interact with any particular person. Two concepts which can help are that of the 'Self-Image' and 'Informal Contract'.

Self-image

We each of us have an image of ourselves. This is formed by our childhood, education, character and experiences. Our image is basically an evaluation of our own abilities, our rightful place in society and the level of our ambitions. And the greater the gap between our self-image and our perception of ourselves in reality, the greater will be our anger, guilt and frustration. The source of many people's dissatisfaction at work and poor performance will frequently be that the reality of their position is not in line with their self-image. The solution will then be either trying to help the person move nearer to their self-image or explaining the unreality of the self-image. Offering more money, appealing to their loyalty or making open or veiled threats will only be counter-productive.

Too often we tend to attribute our goals to other people who may have quite different self-images and motivation to us. A typical example would be when a manager decides to decentralize an operation and give more responsibility to subordinates. This he sees as a positive move as he values challenge and uncertainty. He is therefore surprised when they react negatively because they either do not want, or do not feel they have been sufficiently prepared for the increased level of risk in their jobs. It is important, when dealing with people, to assess what their self-images are. Any suggestions or actions which fit in with these images will fall within that person's zone of comfort. But if you appear to challenge or threaten the self-image, you will usually meet hostility and resistance.

One classification of self-image is into four 'life positions' which are:

'I'm OK, you're OK'

These people are usually optimistic, relate well to others and assume a positive attitude to their life and work.

'I'm OK, you're not OK'

Some people are generally distrusting and suspicious. They may be competitive and ambitious, because they believe they can only satisfy their needs at others' expense rather than through cooperation. Much of Western education and the media encourage this kind of attitude.

'I'm not OK, you're OK'

Often people believe they are victims of circumstances and are envious of others' luck. They may feel inadequate compared to others and even blame others for their own lack of achievement.

'I'm not OK, you're not OK'

There is a group of people who see no value in either themselves or others. They are usually cynical, negative in their relations with others and often resistant to any form of change.

Nobody will ever fall clearly into any of the four categories and people will change depending on their circumstances. However, by trying to picture a person's self-image and classifying it, we can move nearer to understanding how they think and how we should most successfully deal with them.

Informal contract

Another idea, very closely linked to the hierarchy of needs and self-image is that of the 'informal contract'. Most people have a written or formal contract with their employer. However, we also have an unwritten or 'informal contract' which is much broader in scope. The informal contract covers our expectations – we may expect to be treated with respect, to have our opinions taken seriously, to be given challenging or unchallenging tasks, to have interesting work or else repetitive work, which leaves us free to devote our attention to other issues and so on. The organization may expect us to be loyal, to accept management's dictates unquestioningly or else to be free with criticism and ideas, to respect age and seniority or to bring new thoughts and methods. If these unwritten, informal contracts are not in harmony conflict, dissatisfaction, misunderstanding and low performance usually result.

A manager needs to be aware of the wide variety of informal contracts his people may have, when judging how to motivate them or how to encourage them to adapt to and buy-in to any proposed changes. In particular, organizations need to be realistic about the expectations they include in their informal contracts. Few people will ever achieve self-fulfilment from selling hamburgers, working on a production line or selling computers. For an employer to act as if they will, can only cause cynicism and alienation. Organizations must accept that our informal contract with our employers is only one of the many informal contracts we have with the different groups we belong to and it will only satisfy certain needs. But if the organization can go some way towards satisfying these needs, the more innovative and productive its people are likely to be.

Some organizations use fairly old-fashioned methods of motivation

2
The manager's role

The traditional image of the manager was of someone who planned, organized and controlled the work of his subordinates. Though some companies still cling to this view, many others are finding that it is rapidly becoming inappropriate and often unworkable. There are a number of reasons for this:

- Social trends such as higher educational levels, a growth in democracy and participation, and higher expectations of freedom and responsibility conflict with the idea of firm management control.
- Automation and information technology have reduced the number of routine, non-thinking jobs, so few managers now control large numbers of people doing repetitive work.
- Increasingly staff are becoming 'knowledge-workers' who know more than their managers and so management are dependent on their subordinates' goodwill and participation.
- The manager's role has changed from managing stability to management of change. Moreover the pace of change is accelerating meaning that more ideas need to be developed and introduced more quickly than ever before. When Ford brought out the Model T he had a competitive advantage for fifteen to twenty years. When Apple made a similar breakthrough with their first computer, they had less than five years before the competition had caught up. This acceleration has meant that activities have to be carried out simultaneously, rather than in sequence, breaking down the barriers between functions and pushing managers away from being controllers of their own department towards being coordinators of the work of interdepartmental teams.

Too many organizations have not understood either the criticality of the manager's position or the need to adapt to the changing environment. The cost of a manager who, for whatever reason, fails to perform, is not just his salary. It is also all the lost opportunities from demotivating his people, from stifling their potential to contribute and from slowing down any new development due to his department's lack of cooperation. Previously, when different functions such as finance or production worked almost in isolation, the costs of ineffective management were limited. But as different areas are finding the need to move towards closer cooperation, such practices as accepting poor managers or putting them 'out to grass' where they can 'do little harm' are becoming increasingly indefensible.

Clearly the manager's role will change depending on the organization, job, situation and so on. However in order to identify what role the manager should play, it may be useful to consider some ideas, where the manager is seen as a resource to his employees rather than being the authoritarian decision-maker and representative of the organization's power over its members.

Facilitator

This is based on the view that the majority of people are neither stupid nor lazy and will genuinely try to do reasonable work providing the 'system' allows it. The main way of improving an area's effectiveness is not to somehow try to motivate, cajole, bribe or threaten people to try harder. Rather it is to remove all the barriers and constraints which prevent people contributing. Management's job is thus less a matter of controlling and more one of continuously improving the systems in which people work. Some typical cases might be as follows.

Few organizations successfully communicate their overall strategy down to all levels. Being unaware of top management's goals, departments and people will work in what they believe to be the right direction. But their efforts may in fact be either misdirected or even against the organization's overall interests. Another case would be when inappropriate plans are handed down to, for example, a production department, without getting input from the people who will have to carry them out. People will then find themselves forced to work in a way they know is unproductive. Similarly the installation of new equipment or systems is seldom preceded by sufficient consultation with those who will operate them. The result, again, being lower effectiveness and increased frustration with 'the organization'.

One expert suggested that, for most increases in effectiveness, 80 per cent will come from improving the operating systems (tools, work methods, work organization, information flow, strategy, training, quality of management) and only 20 per cent from directly increasing the performance of the people.[1] If these figures are anywhere near the truth, then this places a clear responsibility on management to 'unblock' the organization and allow people to operate to their full potential, instead of blaming attitudes, work practices or lack of interest for any failure to achieve planned results.

Conflict resolver

This idea accepts that there is unlikely ever to be complete harmony of interest between an organization and its members. The organization will usually have one over-riding set of objectives which necessitate different departments and individuals compromising their own aspirations and interests. The organization may want more loyalty, obedience or effort than its members want to give or feel it deserves, while members may want more responsibility, job interest and variety than the organization knows how to provide. The role of the manager then becomes one of trying to resolve in the most constructive way the inevitable tension between organizational and personal goals. This theory suggests that by its very nature any organization will to some extent be an 'oppressive dominant reality' for the people who work in it. The manager will only get the best performance from his people by creating a 'free area of activity' in which they can develop and contribute.

This view tries to go beyond the unrealistically simplistic attitude of some organizations that their members will naturally identify totally with their interests. Instead it accepts that some conflict is inevitable and gives managers the responsibility of recognizing this and finding positive solutions.

Coordinator

Many organizations are discovering that the complexity of the issues they are dealing with is forcing them to develop ways of harnessing the knowledge of different functions at all levels into cross-functional teams. When Western car manufacturers are trying to bring down the development time of a new model from six years nearer to the Japanese average of three years, departments such as design, development, manufacturing and marketing can no longer operate in sequence, where one department 'tosses its work over the wall' into the next function. Instead they are having to work more in parallel, solving manufacturing and marketing problems at the same time as they finalize the basic design. Traditional practices, where cross-functional contact was maintained by one department manager talking to another, are too slow and inflexible to allow this type of development. And as rapid adaptation to a changing environment becomes essential for survival and speed to market becomes the main competitive weapon, the ability to quickly assemble effective cross-functional teams will become even more critical to any organization's success.

In this scenario, the manager is no longer the maker of unilateral decisions. Instead he recognizes that there are some issues where the organization needs to apply a broad range of experience. His task thus becomes one of recognizing which problems have broader implications and deciding which individuals are most likely to be able to contribute to the solution. He has to assemble a task-related team, guide it through to finding (and, if appropriate, implementing) a solution and then disband the team once the task is completed. He is no longer the omniscient leader of the team, but rather is responsible for ensuring the right environment is created for the team to operate effectively. He is a coordinator not a controller.

To some people these three pictures will appear to be common sense, while others will consider them faddish and out of touch with the reality of organizational life. But it could be argued that it is precisely because many organizations are trapped within traditional, unproductive management methods that they react cynically to alternative proposals. Whatever the case, it is clear that in the most successful organizations there is a shift away from the behaviours on the left of the list opposite towards those on the right.

Two Contrasted Management Models	
Controller, bureaucrat, decision-maker	Coordinator, facilitator, guide
Interest in task/results	Interest in people achieving results
Formality	Informality
Authoritarian	Enthusiast
People as an expense to be managed	People as resources to be developed
Rules and regulations	Communicates a vision
Customers/suppliers as opponents	Customers/suppliers as partners
Political skills	Human relation skills
Knows all the answers	Depends on his people's expertise

3
Management style

This has probably been one of the most thoroughly investigated areas of management. Yet also it has probably been one of the most disappointing in terms of giving clear guidance as to what makes a good or bad manager. Whilst many plausible theories and models have been suggested they tend to suffer from two main weaknesses:

1. They usually reflect the political and social trends of the period in which they were developed. So what is considered as exemplary at one time is later seen as reprehensible.
2. They either consider too few variables to be convincing or too many to be useful.

However, it may still be helpful to briefly review some of the work which has been done, before suggesting some management styles and when they may be most appropriate. The research into leadership is generally split into three main periods – trait studies, the behavioural approach and the contingency model.

Trait studies

This approach was dominant in the West from around 1910 to the 1950s. To simplify, its basic assumption was that certain people are born leaders. The studies concentrated on finding out what personality characteristics successful leaders had in common, in order to develop a profile for identifying future leaders.[2] The types of answers reached – a leader needed intelligence, enthusiasm, initiative, integrity, sociability, determination – were too general to be of much use. Moreover, there were too many exceptions to the rule – leaders who did not possess these attributes and yet were successful and leaders who did demonstrate the attributes but were not successful.

The belief that there was a born leadership elite stemmed from a society with two important features. A small group of wealthy people controlled most of the productive resources and most organizations were autocratic, hierarchically structured and dismissive of the aspirations of their members.

The wider distribution of power and spread of democracy has all but discredited anyone who openly supports this theory.

Behavioural approach

This school of thought, which is most often shown by the Blake and Mouton 'management grid', focused less on the characteristics of leaders and more on how they interacted with subordinates.[3] Its proponents believed that people looked for satisfaction of their social and self-actualization needs at work and that by responding to this, an organization could decrease alienation, improve relations and obtain higher productivity. The favoured style proposed was democratic as it was thought that involving people in decision-making, and giving responsibility and autonomy was likely to make them more positive to contributing to the organization. The behavioural school tended to class management style on a scale from authoritarian to democratic, directive to non-directive, or task orientation to people orientation. While this approach fits very much with today's environment, research did identify many exceptions – for example, when a large number of people were doing boring, repetitive work or when rapid change was required to ensure organizational survival. In such cases an authoritarian management was more effective than a democratic one.

The contingency model

This proposed the unsurprising idea that management was effective where the leader's style best matched the demands of the situation.[4] So while a democratic, participative style was productive in some cases, in others it could be inappropriate and an authoritarian approach much more effective. Much of the research concentrated on identifying which situations would be most favourable to which management style.

In reality a manager cannot choose his style in complete freedom. Nor can he switch from one style to another without causing considerable personal stress and confusion amongst those he deals with. In trying to judge what style will be appropriate there are probably about five key constraints he needs to consider:

His own personality

Each of us can adopt several different styles depending on the situation. But we all have a limited repertoire and would find it difficult to maintain a style which was totally unnatural to us for any period of time. We are naturally sociable or distant, enthusiastic or thoughtful, talkative or reserved. We can modulate our basic behaviour but not change it totally.

The organization

Many organizations have a very strong culture or 'house style' which sets clear limits on how managers conduct themselves. Any marked deviation from this will tend to cause pressure to be brought to bear on the manager to conform.

The task

If a task is very simple and clear or else if there are severe time pressures, then clearly a democratic approach is inappropriate. Common examples of this are organization turnarounds, where strong directive management is often neces-sary to deal with years of indecisiveness and organizational drift. Only when effectiveness has been regained can management afford to move towards more democratic styles. On the other hand, with complex tasks requiring a large amount of knowledge input from subordinates a participative approach is most productive.

Needs of subordinates

Many subordinates will want to be involved in planning and decision-making, especially if they are younger and more highly educated. But there are others who may have a low tolerance for ambiguity and may want order and stability. When invited to participate in decision-making, they may feel the manager is paid to deal with problems and that he is trying to avoid his responsibility by involving them.

The organization's environment

If the external environment is reasonably stable, management can be directive. However, if the environment is constantly changing, there is a need both for an effective upward flow of information and for decentralization of decision-making so the organization can respond quickly. In this case a more democratic, participative approach is essential.

While most managers might intuitively tend towards a style which tries to involve subordinates as fully as possible, it is not always clear that the organization, the task, the manager's personality or the subordinates them-selves will always favour this. A manager must, therefore, be sensitive to these five key influences on style to ensure his choice is appropriate for the situation.

Possibly the most decisive factor, in deciding what style an organization adopts towards its members, is its view of human nature. There are two powerful models available which can be helpful in enabling organizations to reassess their attitudes and look for ways to make better use of their people.

Rational/economic, social, and self-actualizing man

Consciously or unconsciously most organizations have developed a view of people which drives the way they treat them. One framework for analysing this is to see people as one of:

- rational/economic: basically passive, driven by the need for money, mainly working because of financial pressures;
- social: as social animals, who develop their sense of worth through their relationships with others, who can be made productive if the organization satisfies these needs but alienated if given work which isolates them from other people;
- self-actualizing: wanting to develop themselves to their full potential, looking for responsibility and challenge at work.

Choosing an appropriate management style is not always easy

The structure, style and systems of most organizations will largely depend on which of the above three views their perception of people is closest to. If man is seen as rational/economic an organization will tend to be highly structured, hierarchical with numerous rules, procedures and controls. Organizations who believe man is social will tend to be paternalistic, apparently interested in employee welfare and less controlled. When man is viewed as self-actualizing structures are usually loose, there is room for individual initiative and there is often use of teamwork, special taskforces and project groups to deal with specific problems.

Theory X and Theory Y

Theory X managers believe that people need to be directed, controlled, rewarded and punished if they are to be productive. Theory Y managers treat people as if they are self-motivated and interested in doing a good job. They look for ways to help people develop and contribute.

Most of us would probably like to think we are Theory Y managers and deal with people as if they are motivated by self-actualization. However, this is far from the truth in a number of organizations. But what is most shocking is that there are many organizations who, perhaps unknowingly, treat people at higher levels (management) according to Theory Y principles, but shop-floor workers in a way closer to Theory X as if these people were somehow a lower order of human beings. Such behaviour can only lead to alienation and dissatisfaction in the work force, conflict with management and low effectiveness.

Choice of style

One way of trying to analyse your own management style might be to ask yourself how your subordinates would class your style. For example, you could try to imagine how a subordinate might describe your area. Four types of environment are given below:

1. Teamwork–consensus–participation
2. Innovation–individual initiative–freedom
3. Security–predictability–job for life
4. Competitive–results oriented–survival of the fittest

(You should assign points up to ten against the four options depending on how closely they resemble your area.)

As most organizations do not change as fast as their environments, managers should not only analyse the degree of fit between their current style and the needs of their area. They should also try and look forward at how their area will change over the next three to five years and what implications these changes will have on choice of style. The figure suggests three basic styles and the situations to which they might be appropriate.

	Authoritarian	**Participative**	**Encouraging freedom**
Task	Simple ————————————→		Complex
People	Low skill ————————————→		High skill
Environment	Stable ————————————→		Unpredictable

Figure 2

4
Increasing employee involvement

For much of this century the main influence on job design was the concept of 'Scientific Management' generally associated with Frederick Taylor. Although there has been a reaction against this since the 1950s, there are many organizations which still apply scientific management principles, often to the detriment of employee satisfaction and productivity.

The key characteristics of scientific management are that work can be broken down into simple elements, studied and timed. A 'best method' can be found for most jobs and productivity against set standards tightly controlled by management. Much production-line work is still based on these ideas. In a society where general levels of education are low and unemployment high, this was an effective method of achieving high productivity. However, as education levels, general prosperity and expectations have risen, people have reacted against the

Shop-floor workers often have a lot to contribute

boredom, frustration and powerlessness they feel doing simple, repetitive work. Some companies have made attempts at job enrichment but often these are generated by management or human resource experts, fail to involve the doers and are seen as new attempts to get more for less.

Valuing the whole person

The first step to any serious attempt to improve job satisfaction, and thus performance, is to seriously believe in each worker as a whole person. Too many organizations, particularly those with large numbers of clerical or manufacturing personnel, still behave as if managers are hired from the neck up and everyone else from the neck down. The assumption is that management make decisions and subordinates are there to carry them out. This both denies the creative potential of people and is an incredible waste of the contribution they could make. The average group of people on any production line or in any shop or office probably have a surprisingly wide range of skills and free time interests, yet at work are treated as if they are incapable of thinking. If an organization believes people can contribute then it will look for ways of helping them, if it does not, it will just try to control them.

Job enrichment

The key question to ask about any job is 'if the person works harder will he become more tired and bored or more challenged and satisfied?' If the answer is the first, then whatever incentive you offer is unlikely to be effective in improving performance. The person will weigh up the offer of money against the increase in fatigue and in most instances choose a work rate which suits him rather than you. In this case, you should start to look for ways of moving from the first to the second situation by trying to find a better fit between the individual's expectations and the characteristics of the task.

It is generally accepted that for a job to be satisfying it must:

- be meaningful, something worth while doing;
- allow the person to experience responsibility for results;
- enable the person to see an end result and get feedback on how well or badly the person, department or organization is doing.

Typical features of rewarding work are variety, some involvement in the planning, having a visible identifiable outcome, allowing some interaction with others and providing some opportunity for learning.

There are two main ways of improving job design:

Horizontal expansion is when you include more activities which previously happened before or after a particular job. For example, making a person responsible for a whole assembly rather than just a part of it, or giving a typist or administrator more contact with customers, inside or outside the organization.

Vertical expansion occurs when the activities of planning and controlling work are devolved to the person who will do the job. Typically this might mean giving a person a group of tasks which they can then plan themselves or training a machine operator to carry out his own preventive maintenance or own (statistical) quality control.

Although different people will have different aspirations and abilities, everyone needs to feel they have some control over their work, some chance of developing and a reasonable amount of contact with other people. Without these you will get frustration, high absenteeism, low morale and inadequate productivity. Yet, in the West, we tend to overlook these needs and design jobs to suit the technology or the organization rather than considering the effects on the people who will do them. Every job has, however, a certain design space which a manager can choose to use if he wants.

Introduction of new technology

Theoretically people and machines are complementary. Machines can carry out repetitive, tiring or dangerous tasks without any variation. Humans can do the planning, thinking and problem-solving which machines are incapable of. Yet in practice this potential synergy is often not achieved and new technologies (machines and computers) are seen as repressive by the work-force. Implementation of new technology provides an opportunity to rethink methods, organization and layout which were created by past decisions. For example, you could reallocate job responsibilities, introduce more flexible working hours, redesign the office or machine layout to improve working conditions or train operators so they learn new skills. But too frequently, the structure already in place is just taken for granted and a major opportunity is lost. In Europe there has been a tendency to design new technology to meet technical and productivity requirements while underestimating the organizational and human issues raised by new systems. The result is the failure of technology to deliver the desired result because people and their needs have not been sufficiently catered for in the implementation process.

A study of advanced manufacturing systems suggested that they were significantly less productive in Great Britain and the USA than in Japan and West Germany. Although in many cases the machinery was similar, countries where they had not thought through how satisfying or otherwise the human being's role would be, had poor results from often large investments. If the new technology is seen as taking away job interest, variety or human contact, firstly this is usually a weakness of management rather than a function of the technology and secondly it will seldom be really successful.

Herzberg's Two-Factor theory

A useful model for understanding some aspects of job satisfaction is the 'Two-Factor Theory of Motivation' proposed by an American psychologist, Frederick Herzberg, in the 1950s. Herzberg divided the features of any job into 'hygiene factors' and 'motivators'. Hygiene factors included such items as pay, working conditions, supervision, company policy and status. Motivators were achievement, recognition, responsibility and personal growth. He argued that the hygiene factors could only either be dissatisfiers or neutral to motivation – if you were content with them, you would not be dissatisfied, but in themselves they were unable to motivate you. The motivators, on the other hand, were areas where management could increase motivation and performance. This fits in quite closely with Maslow's hierarchy of needs (see Chapter 1, Motivation) and reemphasizes the fact that people need more from a job than money, good working conditions or security and that unless management addresses the aspirations for responsibility, growth and independence, then they will fail to get the full potential from their work-force.

Quality circles and work groups

In addition to improved job design, employee satisfaction and contribution can be increased through ideas like quality circles and semi-autonomous work groups. Both of these techniques function well in cultures like Japan, where workers and management both believe that it is in everyone's interest for the firm to create wealth. But in the West, where management and workers have been more focused on outsmarting the other in 'dividing the spoils', if such practices are not introduced properly, they can be memorable failures and even counter-productive.

Quality circles consist of a foreman meeting regularly with a group of workers to look at ways their area can be improved. The target is not just quality but also efficiency, cost and productivity. The philosophy is that by making continuous small improvements you will make massive improvements in the long term. The Western approach seems to be to maintain the status quo as long as possible and then abruptly at the last moment try to make a major change. As well as improving effectiveness, quality circles increase job satisfaction by giving the worker some control over his environment and some participation in decision-making.

Semi-autonomous work groups can be formed by grouping a series of related tasks and giving a group some degree of participation in organizing their work. This gives people some freedom and responsibility and also satisfies their need to belong to a cohesive group. In addition, it is much easier for a manager to monitor the output of four or five groups than that of 25 to 30 individuals.

If there has been a history of tension between managers and the managed, as is the case in many organizations, great care has to be taken with the introduction of any work improvement technique. Otherwise it will only be viewed as another management trick and rejected without reasonable consideration. These techniques always fail when imposed from above in an atmosphere of distrust. For them to work requires a change in attitude from both sides. This takes time and needs a lot of communication and hard work. Most organizations work on a 'need to know' basis and are poor at giving out information. For people to be motivated they should be given enough information so that they can begin to contribute creatively and enough responsibility and reward to feel it was worth the effort.

5
Negotiation

Most people recognize that almost all the contacts we have, especially at work, involve some form of bargaining or negotiation. Even if they are not officially labelled as 'negotiations'. When dealing with bosses, other departments and subordinates, there is normally some give and take from both sides, unless coercion is utilized. So many of the features of achieving successful negotiations can usefully be applied in these contacts.

Identifying common interest

Superficially negotiations involve a conflict of interest. Typical ones would be unions versus management or buyer versus seller. In the West we are brought up to be competitive and are automatically inclined to try and outsmart those we see as our opponents – to be the winner. Too often people enter negotiations with the conviction that one side will win and the other lose – a so-called win/lose situation. In fact if one side is clearly seen to lose, resentment will build up and, the next time the two sides meet, the previous 'loser' will be even more determined to win. So ultimately the relationship turns to confrontation and both sides are losers – win/lose almost inevitably turns into lose/lose.

The Japanese believe that people negotiate in order to find ways of better creating wealth for both parties. This compares to the Western attitude of negotiating the division of a limited cake. If the real aim of a negotiation is the creation of mutual wealth or well-being, then both sides clearly have an interest in coming to an agreement. In fact, very seldom does one party actually enter discussions with the express intention of them breaking down – even though some people may seem to act as if they did. The reason many negotiations are unsatisfactory is that participants fail to understand that, as they are in the business of creating wealth for both of them, their common interests must far outweigh their differences. They then allow the discussion to become adversarial rather than constructive. Essential to a successful negotiation is the recognition of common interest and the use of this to build up a relationship where both sides are working together to solve a problem, rather than seeking to outwit each other.

One idea is that there are two main types of negotiation. 'Positional' is where each side has a firm position and tries to extract concessions from the other. 'Interest bargaining' is where you try to convince people you're all on the same side dealing with a common problem. With 'positional' you risk losing; with 'interest bargaining' both sides gain. In a constructive negotiation you should try to move from positional to interest bargaining so that you are 'hard on the problem, soft on the people'.

Pre-negotiation preparation

First, know yourself. Identify and clarify your own goals and make sure you are honest with yourself about what you want and why. For example, are you going in to ask for price concessions, when what really concerns you is whether the other side can deliver on time, or has the right quality? Or are you about to ask for more money, when the deeper issue is one of job satisfaction? If you ask for the wrong thing, you will never reach a satisfactory conclusion. You should also ensure that you are the right person to handle the negotiation in terms of having both the authority to come to a conclusion and the technical knowledge to deal with any questions.

You will need to establish your maximum supportable position (MSP) and your lowest acceptable result (LAR). The MSP is the maximum you think you can ask for and *support* with facts – unrealistic demands will only weaken your position as you will quickly be forced to climb down and so will lose credibility. Your LAR is the point below which you are better off not dealing. It is important to be absolutely clear about this, otherwise the human and social dynamics in negotiation may push you too far, causing you to make concessions you will later regret. You may also want to clarify your realistic target, the result you expect and are happy to accept.

Next, know your opponent. Try to put yourself in his position. How does he feel about dealing with you? What does he want from you? Why? What are his MSP, LAR and target? What is your common interest? What can you offer him, which is not too important to you, but which he might value?

If there are several of you going into a negotiation, you all need to be clear on your MSP, LAR and targets. You should all have well-defined roles, so you do not give the impression of being divided. You should also practise how you will answer the other side's arguments and identify any weaknesses in your position. Remember, almost never will one side in a negotiation hold all the aces although it may think it does. So you should expect your opponents to come with a powerful case.

Negotiating

You must be sure that you are dealing with the right person, that they have the authority to conclude a deal. You don't 'talk to the monkey, when you could be talking to the organ-grinder'. It is a classic tactic for someone to appear to come to closure and then to say 'I'll just have to check this with . . .'. It leaves them free to come back and ask for more concessions. Above all, if you find you are dealing with the monkey, never make your final offer. You'll need this in reserve when his boss, the organ-grinder, sends him back to ask for more.

Understand whether this will be a one-off meeting or is just part of a process. Particularly, be aware if you will need to maintain a long-term relationship with the person. If this is likely, he may be reacting more to you as a person than to the things you say and he will constantly be asking himself whether he wants long-term relations with someone like you.

In the negotiation always be calm, friendly and logical, never antagonistic – you are looking to make a friend to deal with a common problem. Do not try to browbeat your opponent or ridicule him. You may want to attack his position, but never attack him personally. He will not mind you sinking his arguments, but will bitterly resent any hint of personal criticism. In any negotiation you will simultaneously be dealing on rational, emotional and political levels. You can break down someone else's rational position, but if you appear to pose an emotional or political threat, they will put up resistance which no logical argument can counteract.

Continuously in a negotiation you should not be looking for ways to simply further your own cause. Rather you should be looking for ways to further your cause by finding a range of solutions which have advantages for both parties.

You should avoid saying 'no' or giving an ultimatum as you will only put yourself in a position from which it may be difficult to extricate yourself. If your opponent says 'no' treat this as 'maybe' and always try and keep the negotiation open by use of expressions such as 'but what if . . .?' Because once a negotiation has hit an impasse, it is always more difficult to reopen discussions (as one inevitably has to in life) than if you had kept the door open.

Keep trying to read behind the surface of what your opponent is saying. If he claims 'these are our normal terms', he means he's willing to make a special arrangement. If he insists 'I can't go back to my members with that offer', he's asking you to give him something else, so he can sell the agreement to those he represents. Particularly try to assess whether he is asking for what he really wants. If he requests a lower price, you may make him quite happy by offering a guaranteed delivery date. Too often, money and price reductions are asked for when other factors will provide greater satisfaction.

Throughout, you should be aware that your opponent has to go back to his organization after the negotiation. He does not want to be seen to have failed, so anything you can offer him to help him appear successful will make him more willing to compromise.

After the negotiation

Try to be the last one to make a concession, even if it is only a minor one. It will make your opponent more comfortable with any agreement and easier to deal with the next time. If you feel you have won, never gloat or underline the fact. Sometimes you should even look for issues you don't mind losing in order that both sides feel they have gained something – you may meet again and nobody will allow you to win all the time.

At the end, always recap the position. Also ensure that all agreements and points still to be resolved are written down and review them clearly with your opponents, so there is no room for misunderstanding or manoeuvring later. You may even want to compliment your opponent on being a tough negotiator or, better, tell him you feel that you have achieved a lot together. It costs you nothing to say it and will help considerably to clear the air and to create the environment for a productive long-term relationship.

Other suggestions

- Never be dishonest, if you are found out people will hear about it and you will seriously damage your credibility.
- Try to avoid surprises. You must have well-prepared arguments, but it seldom pays to try and devastate the opposition with some new set of facts. People tend to act emotionally, rather than rationally, to surprise. So however good your information is, you will find it not being accepted.
- Try to talk the other person's language, but without appearing patronizing. People view the world in very different ways depending on their backgrounds. You'll never convince a financial person using a marketing perspective or a union representative by talking about what's good for the company. You must use arguments which fit in with their world view and offer the kind of concessions which they feel are important.
- Sometimes you can avoid the lengthy process of negotiation by simply asking 'what can I offer you for you to leave the room completely satisfied?' When faced with this question many people step down from their position as the 'tough negotiator', lower their defensive barriers and moderate their demands. Then you find you can actually offer them more than they have asked for and still reach a mutually satisfactory conclusion.

6
Transactional Analysis

Transactional Analysis (TA) was mainly developed in the 1950s by an American psychiatrist Dr Eric Berne. It grew out of psychoanalysis and group therapy and was a means of treating individuals who were unable to form relationships with others. However, in spite of its rather specialized origins, TA can be quite a useful tool for helping people understand and improve their interactions with others, both at work and in their private lives.

The theory of Transactional Analysis

TA is a method for analysing the interactions (called 'transactions') between people. Its strengths are that it is simple to understand and easy to apply. Very often, because we have developed certain behaviour patterns over many years, our reactions can be automatic and seemingly inevitable. If our superior reprimands us, we will tend to respond in a predictable way. If one of our staff makes some error, we will likewise usually have a standard response. TA shows that such automatic reactions are not necessary and that we have a great deal of freedom of choice in how any transaction develops. In particular, it emphasizes how important the opening statement in any transaction is for determining the outcome of the interaction.

TA proposes that we have three main states of mind (called 'ego states'), which we continuously move between, depending on our mood and the situation. Each of these ego states will lead to certain patterns of behaviour. This behaviour covers our attitudes, thoughts, language, tone of voice and body language. By identifying and understanding these three ego states and their implications for our interactions with others, we can significantly improve these interactions.

When we start any conversation, we will do this from a particular ego state. We will also be trying to 'hook' the 'complementary' ego state in the other person. If our ego states are complementary, we can often have a successful exchange. If they cross, the interaction is likely to be unsatisfactory and may even lead to conflict.

The three ego states

Parent

This state is a reflection of the attitudes and behaviours of a parent. There are two possible sides to the parent state – the critical parent, who embodies rules and values, and the nurturing parent, who expresses love and concern. The typical behaviours are:

Critical Parent
Attitudes/thoughts: superior, moralizing, dominating, demanding, authoritative, principled
Language: 'you must, you should, why don't you? how can you?'
Voice: raised, demanding, critical
Body language: pointing finger, impatient, frowning, shaking head, crossed arms, tapping table

Nurturing Parent
Attitudes/thoughts: helping, caring, concerned, forgiving, patience, reassurance
Language: 'What can I do to help?, what's wrong?, relax, take it easy'
Voice: soft, calm, slow, relaxed, comforting
Body language: smile, wink, hand on shoulder, slow movements

Adult

This is our rational and unemotional ego state. In it we can analyse facts and figures, solve problems, weigh up various courses of action, take a balanced view of situations.

Attitudes/thoughts: rational, intellectual, logical, analysing options, sensible
Language: 'What exactly happened?, how do you see it?, what reasons would you suggest?'
Voice: calm, neutral, clear, unemotional
Body language: good eye contact, erect posture, alert, interested in others

Child

The child state mirrors the kinds of feelings and emotions which were part of our childhood. As with the parent state, there are two sides to the child – the natural child is uninhibited, spontaneous and emotional, the adapted child is a result of the child reacting to punishments and rewards and is submissive, withdrawn, but also manipulative and vengeful.

Natural Child
Attitudes/thoughts: playful, creative, energetic, inventive, joking, trusting, curious, boisterous, egoistic
Language: 'I feel, do you know what I've discovered?, I wonder if, I wish we could'
Voice: excited, laughing, enthusiastic
Body language: gestures, active, can't sit still, mimicry

Adapted Child
Attitudes/thoughts: subservient, lying, shame, guilt, anger, fear, helplessness, depressive
Language: 'I couldn't care less if . . . , is it all right if I?, why can't I ever?, why is it always me?'

Voice: sour, angry, unstable, pleading, complaining
Body language: embarrassed, self-conscious, biting nails, nervous

Complementary and crossed transactions

In any situation we have a certain amount of freedom to choose which ego state we want to operate in. And this choice will have a major influence on the outcome of our interaction with others. For example, you and a colleague have just given a presentation which did not go as well as you had hoped. You could react by saying something like: 'no matter what we do, they always try to find some holes in it' or 'I don't know why they even bothered to ask us at all'. In both cases you are acting like a sulking, depressed, adapted child and you are throwing out a line hoping to hook a complementary response. Your colleague could reply like another adapted child, 'you're right, and to think of all the work we put in', or could be a nurturing parent – 'don't worry about it, I'm sure we can think of another approach'. Both of these ego states would be complementary to your own and although your communication would not be very productive, it would at least be without friction.

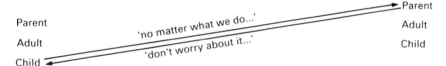

Figure 3 A complementary transaction – child appeals to parent. Parent responds to child

However, your colleague may choose not to accept your invitation for him to respond as a nurturing parent or as another child. Instead he may respond as a critical parent – 'if you hadn't insisted so much on the necessary changes, they might have been more open' or he could be an adult – 'I must admit, I should have gathered more data on the key points, before suggesting such radical change'. Here the transactions are crossed and the interaction will either be stormy or break down quickly.

Figure 4 A crossed transaction – child appeals to parent, but adult responds to another adult

You could quickly improve the transaction, if you moved out of the child into the adult state to respond to your colleague's invitation and said 'I suppose you're right, when should we get together and . . . ?' But if you remained in the child state, obviously little would be achieved.

If, on the other hand, you had opened the exchange in the adult state, and your colleague had responded in the adult state you could have had a useful exchange.

Using Transactional Analysis

Although TA may seem simplistic, it can be a powerful way of examining why some interactions are much more successful than others. If you open an exchange as a nurturing parent or as a critical parent, you will encourage your opposite number to respond as an adapted child. Providing they do, the exchange may be successful, in that the states complement each other, but it will not usually be very productive.

Whereas, if you open as an adapted child you will be calling for another adapted child or a nurturing parent. Providing you receive the required response, the interaction can go on a long time without conflict, but again may not be very productive.

The majority of work can obviously be most effectively conducted in an adult-to-adult mode. If one person is in an adult state and the other in a parent or child mood, less will be achieved. Two critical parents will normally generate a considerable amount of friction. But some types of work, for example creative thinking and problem-solving, may be much more productive, if people can move into the uninhibited enthusiasm of the natural child state. Similarly, when motivating a group, you may find it worth while using some of the characteristics of the natural child.

Many manager/subordinate relationships work on a critical parent/adapted child or nurturing parent/adapted child basis. Such relationships can last many years as the ego states are complementary. But, as shown, they tend not to be particularly productive. Managers or subordinates in such a situation should try and move to an adult/adult if they are to improve their interactions.

Some organizations, particularly those which are very hierarchical and which have rigid control systems, will actively push managers and subordinates into parent/child relations. But if the organization is to try to encourage contributions from its employees and participation in decision-making, it has to break down the parent/child habits and encourage people to work in more adult-to-adult ways.

One way of summarizing TA is to say that the parent *knows*, the adult *thinks* and the child *feels*. The important issue is to be able to use an ego state which is appropriate to a situation and to help those you interact with, to move into ego states which will complement your own and lead to constructive transactions.

GROUPS AND MEETINGS

7 Group formation

8 Group behaviour and roles

9 Negative aspects of groups

10 Effective meetings

Introduction

Estimates of how much time managers spend in meetings vary from between 30 and 50 per cent. Whatever the real figure, meetings represent an extraordinary investment of time and energy – an investment, many people feel, which is not justified by the results. Meetings are more often described as wasted time, pointless and unproductive than as stimulating and effective. But a good meeting can quickly achieve the kind of progress that any individual working on his own could not hope for. Meetings are, unfortunately, much used, abused and misunderstood. In many organizations, the enormous potential of meetings is seldom realized and they remain unproductive and even counter-productive. Meetings and working in groups fit in well with modern democratic ideas about the importance of the individual, participation and shared decision-making. But we do not yet seem to have learned how to use them effectively.

There are two aspects to improving the productiveness of meetings. The first is to develop an understanding of the, often very complex, processes at work when any group forms. The second is to establish a number of actions which can help dramatically improve the effectiveness of any particular meeting. While some of the theory behind group formation may appear a little abstract, our proven lack of success in using groups and meetings productively suggests there is a general need to try and go beyond superficial, quick-fix solutions.

7
Group formation

Formal and informal groups

It is generally accepted that there are two main types of group. Formal groups are those set up by an organization or by the participants to try and achieve certain goals. Formal groups would include task forces, management teams, committees, boards of directors, pressure groups etc. Informal groups are formed by people who have some kind of affinity for each other – they would include workers in a department, people who do similar jobs, people who think in a certain way. The informal group is what a manager comes across when, for example, he tries to make some kind of change in his area and finds there is a kind of united front against it led by 'natural' spokesmen or leaders amongst the work force. The key distinction between the two types is that formal groups are set up to satisfy the needs of the organization, whilst informal groups form mainly to satisfy the needs of their members. Informal groups can be guided towards achieving the objectives of the organization, but if mishandled, they will usually work against them.

It is important for managers to be aware of the existence of informal groups. Whenever they are dealing with any individual above, on or below their level they are also, indirectly, dealing with the informal groups that person belongs to. A common example of the influence of the informal group is when management sets certain performance standards and the workers either openly or by tacit agreement set their own standards, which are often below management's targets. If management offer performance incentives, the individual will be torn between responding to them or conforming to informal group pressure not to break ranks. Usually, loyalty to the informal group wins. So if management want to improve productivity, they have to find ways (for example participation in target-setting) of moving the whole informal group's goals closer to their own. One theory is that we all work under a dual control and reward system, where there is constant tension between the demands of our superiors and those of our informal group.

The formation of formal groups

Most of our time in meetings will be spent in formal groups and it is with these that we seem to have the most difficulty making the event productive. It is in fact unrealistic to expect a formal group to function effectively shortly after it is put together. Many studies have shown that there is a complex process most groups go through before they begin to perform. The members have to get to know each other, assess each other's strengths and weaknesses, examine their task and the likelihood of the group completing it successfully, look for people with something in common and those who might be threats, find out who will be the natural leader and if this will be the formal leader, develop ways of operating and resolving the inevitable differences of opinion. And the final effectiveness of any group is directly related to how successfully it deals with the issues arising during its development.

There are several models of how groups form, most of which identify between three and five main stages. One of the most useful is called Tuckman's Integrative Model, which proposes four main phases. These have been named 'forming, storming, norming and performing'. Alternatively these four phases can be seen as the group's birth, childhood, adolescence and maturity.

Birth (Forming)

At this point people will be polite and careful. The real group has not yet formed. Instead, there is just a collection of individuals testing each other out. The general mood will be one of watching how other people behave to find signs of what will be expected. People will generally feel torn between being inhibited about openly expressing any strong views and yet at the same time wanting to create a certain impression. The group may make some decisions about how and when to meet but are unlikely to be able to make any progress with their main task.

Childhood (Storming)

The group starts to get down to work. Quite quickly the initial consensus breaks down and differences begin to emerge. These differences can be over how to approach the task, how to complete it, what sort of people or skills may be necessary and even what the real task is. For example, if a group was given a broad task like improving profitability, service or quality, it is likely the members would all have radically differing definitions of where the problem lay, reflecting their various backgrounds.

There may also be personality problems. Some people will want to attack the task immediately, others will favour a more formal approach. Some may believe they know the solution and these 'solutions' may be in conflict. People will begin to look for support and the group may start to split up into opposed sub-groups. It is at this point that 'hidden agendas' start to come out. These are the personal interests each individual may be hoping to satisfy. Usually they stem from his position and loyalty to the function where he normally works (as there is not yet any loyalty to the group) and commonly they are at variance with the interests of the others and of the group as a whole.

Leadership is another issue which often comes under question. It may be felt that the original formal or natural leader's style, views or approach do not fit in with the group's. Or else someone may simply make a bid for leadership causing the others to choose sides.

This stage is normally marked by conflict over one or several key issues. Some people may become disheartened by this and withdraw either mentally or physically. Others will become frustrated with the group's lack of progress and start to behave in negative ways. Yet the storming stage is one which almost every group will go through. Its duration and severity usually depend on the awareness and skill of the chairman and the members to resolve, at least temporarily, their differences. One way of doing this is to choose some smaller, less controversial aspect of the group's task and, by working on this, move the group gradually away from conflict towards cooperation.

Adolescence (Norming)

As the group works together they begin to develop norms – how they will organize themselves, how they will behave, how conciliatory or aggressive they will be, what roles different members will play, what values and aims they will have. Most of these norms are not openly expressed. They develop naturally from the interactions and are tacitly understood by those involved. But once they are arrived at and accepted the group can start really dealing with the task at hand rather than being distracted by all the personality and behavioural conflicts.

Many groups fail to proceed through the storming to the norming phase. If they have not fully resolved the initial conflicts, each time a critical issue arises, all the submerged differences of personality and style reappear. Their energy is then diverted to reliving old battles rather than dealing with the issue at hand. It is not uncommon for groups to hover between storming and norming, with the members aware that something has gone wrong, but unable to break free of the apparently recurrent periods of disagreement.

If new members join the group, this can also hinder the group's development. Not having been through the storming phase they may start to question the norms and methods which have been arrived at, and so drag the group back to a new phase of conflict. This can be avoided if someone from the group has managed to prepare the newcomer by explaining the status the group has reached.

Maturity (Performing)

Only once the group has worked through most of their main conflicts and accepted behaviour norms can it begin to function effectively. At this stage the members begin to help each other, build on each other's ideas and tolerate differences. Strong bonds start to form as the group feels they are achieving something and a sense of group identity forms.

The key issue for managers, as part of or responsible for a group, is to move through to maturity as rapidly as possible. In particular, they must be on the look-out for the group becoming trapped between the second and third stages. Awareness of the different stages can help them understand the processes they are involved in and better deal with the problem of making the group productive.

8
Group behaviour and roles

Reasons for using groups

There are a number of things a group can do more effectively than a set of individuals. These include bringing together different skills and knowledge for problem-solving and decision-making, increasing commitment by involving more people in a task, negotiation and resolving disputes, testing the practicability of a decision. But some organizations are dishonest, when they set up groups, and use them for giving the appearance of action while delaying a decision, for diluting responsibility or for rubber-stamping decisions which have already been made. When an organization is dishonest in this way, people quickly see through it and the group members become distrustful, demotivated and even obstructive. Some groups don't even have a real purpose – they just meet regularly because they have always done so. Having no real task to become involved with, they tend to spend their time discussing trivia or creating unnecessary work to justify the group's existence.

Required and emergent behaviour

Groups satisfy many human needs. For example, using Maslow's hierarchy of needs (see Chapter 1, Motivation) groups can help people fulfil their social, self-esteem and self-actualization needs – they give us something to belong to, an arena where we can establish a position, meaning and respect, and a vehicle for developing ourselves through achieving goals. If a group starts to function well, then often it will move towards satisfying the needs of its members, sometimes at the expense of those of the organization. Two types of group behaviour have been identified – 'required' and 'emergent'. Required behaviour is what the organization specifies – the group should meet so often, cooperate and achieve the goals of the organization. Emergent behaviour is what happens in reality. This may be the same as required. But often group members start to feel a greater affiliation towards the group than to the organization in general. They may begin to unite in disagreeing with the organization's definition of the task, they may think that the organization has misjudged the situation and that they, with their more detailed knowledge, have a better idea of what is going on, or they may just be dissatisfied with the organization or its management and use the group as a means of expressing this dissatisfaction.

When emergent behaviour starts to deviate from required, the group leader must be capable of recognizing this. He must then decide whether he should alter his expectations and trust the group to deliver the expected results or whether the group has gone off at a tangent and needs to be brought back into line. Very controlled, hierarchical organizations frequently find that groups will start to rebel against tight control and challenge the system, whereas looser, more participative organizations will be able to tolerate and benefit from emergent behaviour, even if it diverges from required behaviour.

Task, maintenance and personal behaviour

This is another way of analysing behaviour in groups. It can be a useful model to help understand group dynamics and identify why a group is or is not functioning well. 'Task' behaviour is directed at achieving the objectives the organization has set for the group. 'Maintenance' behaviour is aimed at preserving the group through creating the right atmosphere, compromising to avoid conflict and trying to ensure that everyone is involved in the discussions. 'Personal' behaviour is when one person pursues his own goals at the expense of the others – this may be trying to impress them, diverting them to areas which interest him or away from areas where he is uncomfortable, continuously attempting to be humorous, monopolizing the discussion or trying to score points off others.

Clearly if there is an excess of maintenance behaviour in a group, all the members may feel good about being part of the group, but this may be at the expense of achieving the task – for example, when conflicts are continuously avoided at all costs, this may prevent real progress being made. If there is too much personal behaviour, then time and energy is wasted as people become distracted from the task at hand and usually little is accomplished. The success of the group will depend on being able to balance these three styles of behaviour, so that the group relations remain reasonably harmonious, the members feel they are being appreciated and respected and that enough attention is paid to completing the task.

Roles in groups

Most of us have a preferred role, one which we normally adopt when in a group. This may be as ideas man, organizer, expert, devil's advocate, time-keeper, humorist or whatever. We also have a secondary role – if someone else is playing our preferred role better than we can, rather than compete, we tend to move into this secondary role. It can sometimes be helpful for a manager to think about what his and other people's preferred and secondary roles are.

Research into the roles people play in groups has suggested that the most effective group will not necessarily be one made up of the 'greatest minds'. What was at least as important as ability was that there should be a good balance between the different roles. In experiments, groups of 'experts' tended to be outperformed by groups with a more varied selection of people. Tests done in the 1970s by Dr R. Meredith Belbin in Britain suggested that there were eight

It is healthy to have a variety of viewpoints in a group

main roles people could adopt in groups and that the most successful groups were those where these eight roles were best represented and balanced.[5] The roles are:

Chairman: leads and coordinates the group's efforts. His strengths are not creativity, but rather discipline and focus. He can listen and communicate well and is prepared to work through others and not seek glory for himself.

Shaper: is dominated by the task and shapes how the group approach it. He can be dominant, anxious, energetic, and passionate but also irritable and quickly frustrated by people who disagree. He feels the group is like an extension of his own self and constantly drives it towards action.

Plant: is intellectual and a source of ideas. Possibly the most creative and intelligent in the group, he is interested in concepts not details and can be quickly offended if he feels his input is being criticized. He needs to be carefully handled; otherwise he may withdraw and his creativity be wasted.

Monitor/Evaluator: has an analytic rather than creative intelligence. He can assimilate data and detect the flaws in the proposals. He can prevent the group becoming too carried away by enthusiasm, but can also risk being too critical and thus demotivating the others.

Resource investigator: normally popular, relaxed, with a lot of contacts he can use to assist the group. Tends to work in brief bursts of enthusiasm and has little interest in detail or routine work.

Company worker: likes stability and structure and works to organize the group, developing plans and schedules. An administrator rather than a leader.

Team worker: tries to ensure the group works well together. He mediates during conflict and tries to sort out disagreements. He does not try and grab attention, but rather listens to and encourages others.

Finisher: is highly conscious of time pressures. He may seem impatient as he tries to hurry the group along. His anxiety and insistence may make him unpopular, but he is essential if the group is to meet its deadlines.

There are many variations on these roles and perhaps people do not fall exactly into one or other of them. However there is one important point being made. We may believe that a group of 'experts' or like-minded people will be effective and we may be uneasy over the conflict which occurs when there are many different types of person in a group. But in terms of arriving at the best, most comprehensively thought-out results, a balance of these different roles is more likely to be successful, than when members of a group all think in similar ways.

9
Negative aspects of groups

Some years ago the board of directors of a major European company made a decision to invest over £40 million in two new factories. These were eventually built but never went fully into production as it turned out there was no real requirement for them. The result was that the money was wasted and several hundred jobs lost. At the time of the decision there was an impressive amount of evidence that there was no need to build the factories, yet the directors, all able and experienced people, somehow went ahead with a course of action which several of them knew to be wrong.

Groups should theoretically provide a forum where people with differing backgrounds and experience can come together to generate ideas, take advantage of the variety of opinions and make optimum decisions – decisions which none of the members could have arrived at alone. Yet sometimes this patently does not happen – in fact, there are many cases where the decisions made by groups can seem to those outside to defy both reality and common sense. There are several reasons why even the most able and best informed groups can apparently go completely astray. Awareness of them can help a group identify them when they occur and thus avoid them.

Conformity

When any person joins a group, a process of 'socialization' takes place. The individual tries to find out what types of behaviour are expected in the group and adjusts his own behaviour closer to that of the group. In a way the group 'educates' any new member to accept its norms and ways of thinking. Sometimes this process can be quite subtle and the person unaware it is happening, sometimes (joining an army regiment or sports team) it can be quite open, often including initiation rituals.

This is not to say we lose our independence. But what it does mean is that there is a change of perception and behaviour towards that of the group. If we are faced with an issue where there is uncertainty and where we lack personal experience, we will tend to shift our opinions in line with those of the others in the group in the belief that the group cannot be wrong.

If we do feel that a group decision is wrong, we find ourselves in quite a difficult situation. We may lose confidence in our position and abandon it in favour of the group's. Or else we may decide the issue is not important enough to have a confrontation over and we remain silent, though silence in a group situation is often construed as agreement, so we have, in a sense, agreed to something we know to be wrong. If the individual does decide to stand up for his position several things can happen. The group may be prepared to listen to the person's opinion and adjust its decision if it is convinced. But more commonly the group may be under time pressure, or else several members may believe strongly in, and have vested interests in, the decision made. Then the group starts to put pressure, usually unconsciously, on the individual with comments like 'if we start to discuss that again we'll never get finished' or 'I thought we'd already agreed to . . . ' or 'shouldn't you have brought that up earlier?'

Many people will back down at this stage, preferring compromise and harmony to a battle where they feel they are outnumbered anyway. But if the person persists in raising an objection, the group pressure may become more open with other members saying things such as 'what's up with you today?' or 'oh no, not that again?'

It takes quite a strong character not to feel guilty about wasting the group's time and persist with the case. Should the person persist on contradicting the group the others may become overtly hostile. They may tell the person to stop causing trouble. Or they may use procedural points to cut short the interruption. The use of procedure to deal with 'troublemakers' is very common at events like local political party meetings or annual shareholders meetings. Then claims like 'a vote has been taken so we can move on' or 'the accounts have been audited, so there is no point raising those kind of issues' are used to over-ride possibly embarrassing questions.

Further persistence may lead to the person being screened out, either psychologically or physically. Or else the situation can become like a courtroom where the others sit like judges and ask the deviant to account for his behaviour and his information base. And all the time the individual will have to weigh up the importance of the issue against the importance of being rejected by the group and damaging his long-standing working relationship with the others. It may even become a question of survival in the organization. Usually the issue is sacrificed and the group decision, whether right or wrong, is adopted.

Lack of information and ownership

Like all of us, a group is forced to operate in a situation where it only has imperfect information both about the present and about likely future developments. When this is the case, competing strategies or courses of action often look similar and eventually the group, like any individual manager, will make a decision based often as much on judgement as on knowledge. Having chosen a certain course the group will start to follow it through – in a sense they have 'planted their flag' on that decision and will feel a certain degree of ownership. As the decision is implemented, changes in the environment may begin to throw up doubts about the correctness of the original choice. A flexible group will be able to review the decision and, if necessary, take corrective action. But a more common reaction is for group members to see criticism of the decision as criticism of the group itself. The group then finds it has moved into a position where it is forced to defend its decision. And the stronger the evidence against the decision the stronger will be the group's defence.

Satisficing

The word is a combination of 'satisfy' and 'sufficient' and describes the situation whereby a group tends to adopt a course of action which seems satisfactory and sufficient rather than one which they believe to be the best possible choice. In some cases, for example under intense time pressure or in a group where there is a tendency towards conflict rather than conformity, this may mean adopting the first proposal which isn't murdered. Or else, in a group marked by conformity the lack of discussion may lead to 'satisficing' rather than an objective attempt to review all the options and choose the one which gives the best results or 'optimizes'. The unwillingness to take risks can also lead to 'satisficing'.

Groupthink

Groupthink is a frequent characteristic of group work, which was identified by a researcher called Irving Janis after studying how several 'disasters' in American foreign policy occurred.[6] These included the 'Bay of Pigs' invasion of Cuba and the escalation of the Korean and Vietnam wars. 'Groupthink' is most likely to occur when a group has reached the 'maturity' stage. The members have learnt how to work together, they feel comfortable and productive in the group and they have a sense of belonging and affinity with the others. At this point a number of things begin to happen.

Invulnerability: as the group is functioning well, it begins to become over-optimistic, fails to take notice of warnings that certain decisions may be wrong and feels a certain invulnerability. It tends to explain away rather than discuss evidence which goes against its ideas.

Stereotyping: it often tends to stereotype people outside the group as the 'others', who don't understand or appreciate the group's work.

Conformity: groupthink occurs most where the group members share similar backgrounds and beliefs and so will think in similar ways. If there are discordant voices, pressure to conform along with implicit or explicit threats of ostracism will usually silence them.

'Groupthink' is perhaps the most common at the higher levels of company or organizational management where group members have had similar career paths, have similar interests and are under great pressure not to 'rock the boat'. The decline and/or disappearance of many British manufacturing, service and retailing companies since the 1960s can in part be explained by 'groupthink' – in spite of enormous changes in their competitive environment, their managements collectively deluded themselves into ignoring all the evidence which they found unpalatable.

Political manipulation

Sometimes groups move towards making decisions which have a political rather than rational motivation. Here people with vested interests have been active (between meetings) lobbying the more influential figures in the group. So when the members do meet, there is great pressure put on any objectors to fall into line or else fall out of favour with those in power.

Group survival

Generally when people join groups they feel a sense of loyalty to the area they have come from and they bring with them their 'hidden agendas' – the decisions they want taken which best further the interests of their particular sections. However, if the group reaches maturity this loyalty tends to be transferred to the group, till eventually the group starts to take decisions which are, openly or otherwise, in the group's interest rather than benefiting the organization as a whole. Thus groups set up for a temporary period seem to find reasons for remaining, till eventually they become a fixed feature, whose real purpose and contribution are unclear or forgotten. The existence of the group becomes its rationale.

To go back to the example at the start of this section: one outspoken individual had negotiated what he believed to be a favourable contract with the firm who would build the factories. He had worked hard on the matter, developed a good relationship with the contractors and staked his reputation on the deal. In between the series of meetings which led to the decision, he managed to bring the chairman on to his side. This put pressure on the waverers to fall into line. A couple of objectors still held out. They were accused of wasting time. When they asked for a fuller set of figures, they were told that all the figures had already been fully analysed so there was no need to go through all that again. Their final resistance was met with exhortations to work together and for the whole group to show a common front and come to some agreement. At this point the attitudes of the others were openly hostile. The deviants gave way, the decision was made and the money wasted.

Here most of the negative aspects of groups came into play, causing otherwise intelligent people to agree to something they felt was probably wrong.

10
Effective meetings

Most people's experience indicates that meetings cannot just be allowed to follow their own natural course. The result is usually time-wasting, lack of clear decisions, or bad decisions and frustration with a minority of participants hogging the limelight, talking a lot and saying very little. Meetings need organizing if they are to be productive. Probably the amount of effort you invest in ensuring a meeting is effective will depend on how important the result is to you. But badly run meetings, even if about less vital subjects, will reflect on you and lower other people's opinion of your abilities. Therefore there may be advantages in applying some better meeting disciplines not only to formal group meetings, but also to the informal two- and three-person ad hoc meetings you are involved in as part of the normal working day.

Planning

Objectives: all meetings should have a clear and realistic set of objectives.

Participants: these should be decided not by 'those who regularly attend', but rather by those who are relevant to achieving the objectives. The choice of participants should thus be task-based.

Agenda: there should be a logical agenda aimed at accomplishing the objectives. This should be sent to all participants at least twenty-four hours before the meeting. Some people believe it's best to deal with the most important issue first, while participants are fresh and have time and energy. Another approach is to put a couple of easy items first to generate team-working and momentum, then deal with the key issue. The main item should not normally be left to the end, as by then participants are often tired or thinking about what they will be doing after the meeting. Or else there isn't enough time left to do justice to the main reason for meeting in the first place.

Information: giving out information in a meeting wastes time, firstly while it is being given out, read and digested and secondly while participants analyse it and work out how to react to it. If the distribution of information is necessary to the meeting objectives, this should happen before the meeting so people have already understood it and prepared their responses.

Pre-presentation: if it is a key meeting, you will probably want to meet with all the participants individually prior to the meeting to explain your aims and tactics, and to get their input. In particular you should be on the look out for any 'hidden agendas' they may be bringing to the meeting. These can then be dealt with in the pre-presentation or if this is not possible, at least you will be prepared when they start shooting.

Tactics: meetings, like most human contacts, will function on three main levels – rational, emotional and political. To prepare only your facts for dealing with the rational interaction would be to neglect two-thirds of what will go on in the meeting. You must also think through who will be there, what they will want, what they feel about the other participants, and what they stand to gain or lose. If your proposals necessitate that someone will lose position or power, how can you offer them something so their emotional and political resistance does not sink the whole idea? How can you create a situation in which everyone is seen to win?

Most managers could improve their presentation skills

Proposals: if the group are expected to come up with a solution to a problem, try and prepare one or more draft proposals. It is always easier for people to adapt and build on a proposal than it is for them to work in a vacuum.

During the meeting

Balance: try to ensure a balance between the amount of 'airtime' the different participants take. Also you should balance the time spent on task (achieving the objectives), maintenance (ensuring the group works together well) and personal (allowing people to feel they are contributing and appreciated) activities.

Delegate: at different times it may not be possible to take a decision because of lack of information or because the person who will implement the decision is not present. Often groups will discuss the matter and speculate on the various possibilities. You should try and stop the speculation, delegate someone to find the information or talk to the person involved and then move on to the next point.

Avoid surprises: nobody likes to be surprised, especially not in front of others. People react to surprise emotionally, not rationally. And emotional objections are far more difficult to overcome than rational ones. While it may appear gratifying, in the short term, to 'drop a bomb', it will usually generate resentment and distrust rather than admiration.

Headline first: if people want to make a contribution there are two ways they can do this. They can build up to the conclusion by first explaining all the detail and reasoning. Or they can give the conclusion briefly ('headline') then clarify how they reached it (if necessary). In the first case the listeners use their energy trying to understand where the speaker is heading. In the second, by knowing the conclusion, they can immediately start to build on and develop the idea. By 'headlining' your conclusion first, you make the best use of the group's creative energy.

Features of a successful meeting: sometimes it can be useful to write up on a flip chart a few characteristics of good meetings (or 'ground rules'). By having everyone agree to these at the start, you can refer to them, when necessary, throughout the meeting to keep it productive. The ground rules might include: headline conclusions first, be brief and give explanations only when asked, if you want to criticize an idea first say what you like about it, attack the problem not the people and so on.

Come back to problems: if you appear to hit an impasse, it is more likely to be due to emotional and political rather than rational causes. If so, shelve the problem and move on to a less contentious issue. You may find that once you have got up some momentum again, with the group working together, you can return to the previously irresolvable disagreement and find a solution more easily.

Negative aspects: continuously look out for negative behaviour like groupthink, political manipulation, satisficing and conformity. If these are happening and you cannot stop them, it may be better to stop the meeting and try to deal with the issues in another way.

Ending a meeting

Assign activities throughout the meeting; at the end of each point on the agenda, you should summarize the decision taken, who is to do what and by when. At the end, you should once more summarize all decisions and assigned activities.

Minutes should be brief, list the main decisions and what activities have been assigned, and state who is responsible and by when they must be completed. The minutes should be distributed to all participants within twenty-four hours.

Benefits and concerns: sometimes it can be useful to take five minutes at the end of a meeting and ask the participants to quickly discuss the following three points:

1. Benefits of the meeting – what was achieved? Do they feel people worked well together? Was it worth holding it?
2. Concerns – what more do they think should have been accomplished? Could people have worked together better?
3. What could be done better next time in order to have a more productive meeting?

This tends to heighten participants' awareness of their behaviour and their use of the meeting time and generally leads to a marked improvement in meeting effectiveness in the future.

Follow-up: if it has been an important meeting where major, possibly quite political, decisions have been made, you should meet individually with each of the participants afterwards to get feedback on how they feel things went and any concerns they might have.

Informal meetings

We often underestimate the increased value we could gain from improving our use of informal meetings. Informal meetings are the contacts we have during each day, with one or two people at a time to discuss issues as they arise. Frequently we call people up asking to see them without telling them why, what information they'll need with them and how long we think the meeting will take. Or else we answer our phone and deal with other issues while people are sitting in our office – this is impolite, wastes their time, interrupts the discussion and sends a clear signal to them about how unimportant we think they are. By telling people why we want to see them, specifying the likely duration, giving them our attention and trying to conclude each meeting with a decision, we can significantly raise the quality of these daily contacts and people's estimation of our management abilities.

THE NATURE OF ORGANIZATIONS

11 Organization structure

12 Changing organization structure

13 Organizational culture

14 Organizations as political systems

15 Power in organizations

11
Organization structure

In theory an organization's structure is designed to help members of the organization attain the organization's objectives. Though often structure seems to be actively hindering this and people spend time and effort building up elaborate informal systems to try and work round the official channels. Structure should be a means of organizing resources, clarifying roles and responsibilities, and shaping decision-making and communication procedures. But, if it is inappropriate, it can end up causing conflict and lack of coordination, increasing costs with unnecessary levels in the hierarchy, slowing down information flow and decisions and spreading frustration and demotivation.

In this section, 'organization structure' is not just the position of the various boxes on the organization chart. It also includes the systems, processes and procedures the organization uses for coordinating and managing the work done by the people represented by the boxes.

Control versus trust

Any organization structure is a compromise between two opposite pressures. Different experts have called these opposites uniformity and diversity, control and trust, mechanical and organic, centralization and decentralization, tight and loose. There are pressures on any organization to impose standardization and centralized authority in order to reduce costs through economies of scale, to police the members' activities, to monitor information and to retain senior management control of the use of resources. At the same time there are pressures towards decentralization and delegation of power to push responsibility and accountability down to middle management, to be more flexible and responsive to changes in the environment and to increase motivation and commitment amongst the members. Achieving the right balance between these two opposing forces is critical to any organization's success.

Classical structure

It is probably worth reviewing the principles of what is known as a 'classical' structure or 'bureaucracy'. This is because, although this form is increasingly coming under attack and numerous companies are trying to move away from it, it still tends to dominate many large and medium-sized organizations. The classical organization is based on a military 'command and control' structure. It has a strict hierarchy, clearly defined roles and responsibilities for each level, formal procedures and relationships, and unity of command (each person has only one direct superior). In a classical structure the role is more important than the person who fills it. The freedom and discretion of the individual is strictly limited and creativity or individualism are usually seen as disruptive. There is also a separation of policy-making and administration – those at the top make the major decisions and those below carry them out. In it, loyalty and length of service tend to be rewarded more than contribution and ability.

The classical structure is most obvious in monopolies or near-monopolies, Government departments and large companies with very simple operations (e.g. distribution of oil, fast-food chains, mass production manufacturing). But a significant number of other companies continue, not always appropriately, to display many of its features. For example the claim made by many businessmen and politicians that 'management have the right to manage' owes much to the principles underlying the classical model.

The behavioural approach

In the 1970s, there was a strong movement against classical structures. They were criticized for giving the lower levels virtually no control of their work environment and causing them to feel powerless, apathetic and alienated. It was also proposed that they stifled people's development by taking decision-making away from them, thus keeping them in a kind of immaturity. The new theory was that people should be given more freedom and responsibility, more participation in decision-making and more control over their lives. This, it was claimed, would increase employee satisfaction and thus stimulate creativity and productivity. One way of achieving this was through decentralization into strategic business units (SBUs) and profit centres.

Some of these exercises in devolving power were very successful. But others were clear failures which led to great disruption, yet no marked improvement in morale or output. There are a number of reasons for such failure. One common instance was when corporate management created SBUs which in reality did not have the authority to decide their own destiny. When tested, the centre found itself unwilling to relinquish control. Another frequent scenario was when career-ladder bureaucrats, used to a stable, predictable environment, were suddenly informed that they were now responsible for a level of decision-making for which they had neither the preparation nor the experience. A third example was the attempt to split into separate SBUs organizations which logically formed one entity. By giving different parts the goal of maximizing profit, corporate management could, in this case, create a situation when what was best for individual SBUs was not necessarily best for the organization as a whole.

Contingency theory

This proposes the commonsense view that there is no one correct way to structure an organization.[7] A loose participative structure is not necessarily better or worse than a tight autocratic one, it just happens to be more effective in particular situations. The contingency theory suggests that the choice of structure is dependent ('contingent') on the particular circumstances the organization is in.

The main determinants of structure are the task, the type of people who will perform it and the environment they operate in. The table relates type of structure to these three determinants.

	Tight Structure	*Loose Structure*
Task	Simple, repetitive Known technology	Complex, changing Changing technology
People	Low innovation, passive, efficiency important	Independent, creative, new solutions important
Environment	Stable or controlled by the organization, predictable	Changing, unstable, unpredictable

In a mass-production operation, with a known technology, in a stable environment, there is little room for a trusting, participative structure. The task is limited and efficiency is the main competitive weapon. When management have tried to devolve power in such a situation it usually failed, as it was not appropriate. The nature of the task precluded a democratic approach. On the other hand, many large, bureaucratic organizations have failed, in spite of massive investments, to innovate new products because their heavy control mentality has not permitted their research and development people the freedom they need to be productive.

The contingency theory says that it should be the task which determines the structure. However, in reality, structure is often a product of the past – both its technology and its leaders – and thus can be inappropriate and prevent people from working effectively.

Differentiation and integration

A major contribution of the contingency theory was that by making the task the major driver of structure, it highlighted the need for different structures within one organization. Many organizations seem confused by their internal differences – sales are at war with production; finance can't understand research and development; central office is seen as a useless burden by divisions. Yet it is obvious that different functions have different goals, time horizons, types of people and working practices. This being the case, there is a need to ensure that each department has an appropriate structure – most likely different from the others. There should be 'differentiation' between the areas.

The issue for the organization is not to try and give all departments the same structure and operating procedures. Instead it should try to find ways of ensuring that these 'differentiated' areas, with their variety of styles and structures, can work together to achieve the organization's objectives. It must 'integrate' these 'differentiated' functions. There is a tendency in organizations for different functions to exist in a state of permanent hostility. Each department seems dismissive of the opinions and contribution of the others. In these cases the organization has failed to find ways of assisting the functions firstly in understanding each other, and secondly in learning how to cooperate positively. Variety, working constructively together, rather than centrally-imposed conformity is how an organization can function effectively. A centrally-imposed uniform structure may well suit some departments, but will be completely inappropriate to others.

12
Changing organization structure

Reorganizations appear to have become increasingly popular in the last fifteen years or so. Some companies seem to reorganize every three or four years, some even more often as if in search of an elusive Holy Grail – the 'perfect organization'. Yet one of the more telling comments on management's obsession with reorganization was made nearly two thousand years ago and is commonly attributed to a Roman named Petronius. He wrote:

> We trained hard – but each time we began to work effectively as a group, we were reorganized. I learnt later in life that we have a tendency to meet each new situation with reorganization and also what a wonderful method this is of giving the illusion of progress when it only results in chaos, ineffectiveness and demoralization. *(Gaius Petronius, AD 66)*

(It is worth including this quote just to remind people that the organizational issues we are dealing with today differ very little from those which have confronted many other generations.)

One reason for some managements' urge to reorganize is probably a belief that by making changes in the formal reporting relationships (moving the boxes of the organization chart around) they will improve the organization's results. Experience normally shows that this approach is too shallow and ends in disappointment.

Consistency

As stated in the previous section, organization structure is not just the official responsibilities and reporting relationships. It is also the systems and processes which enable the structure to function. These systems and processes include how strategy is developed and communicated, how people are acquired, trained and developed, how information is communicated and how decisions are made. These systems and processes need to be in alignment with the reporting structure if the structure is to function well.

There are two common management mistakes. One is to identify problems which come from a mismatch between systems and reporting structure and believe the solution is a reorganization. An example of this would be when a research and development department is working in a specialized area, but the personnel policy is to take on X graduates a year and put them through a two-year general graduate training programme. So research and development are never able to get the specialized experts they need. The other mistake is to change the reporting structure without also changing the supporting systems. For example, one company decided to make production workers responsible for checking the quality of their own work. But they kept the old bonus system which rewarded workers only for total output. Similarly a company decided to give divisional managers full profit and loss responsibility, but then continued to insist that they bought certain products from other divisions of the same group, and that a central function kept control of new product development.

In these three cases the systems actively worked against the new reporting structures. Very often the problems of an organization stem not from the wrong structure, but from the failure to ensure that the official organization chart and the systems and processes used are consistent and support, rather than contradict each other.

An example of reorganization

An example of a reorganization which takes into account the tasks to be accomplished, the structure (and systems) relevant to that task, and the need to differentiate and integrate functions might be as follows:

A company wants to find a way of reducing the time taken to develop and introduce new products. Some of the issues to be resolved are: who should be responsible for development, how they can adapt new product ideas to different

There are a number of ways of changing organization structure

factories in different markets, and how they can free the new product development section from the restrictive effects of regular budgetary control while ensuring it still gave value for money.

As there is only a limited number of basic technologies behind the product range, it may be decided to centralize all technology research. This brings the best people in technology together and makes most use of expensive development and test equipment. This section works on a ten-year horizon so annual budgeting and monthly reviews of project status against plan give a satisfactory level of management control. Within this section there is a new venture unit, for each new product idea, headed up by a product champion who is responsible for taking the product all the way through to the market. This ensures that there is someone who has 'ownership' of every new product.

Once the prototype products are developed, they have to be customized to suit individual customer or market requirements. This task is given to each division as they are the most expert in their market areas. There is much tighter control on this stage of the development, as the work has to be coordinated with customers' own product introduction programmes.

Finally the new products are handed over to production where they will be managed within a strict, formal hierarchy. The concern now is hitting daily production and quality targets.

Integration is achieved by two methods. There are clear criteria defining when each part of the operation should hand a product over to the next stage. (Delays in the past have been caused when people good at concept development started to dabble in designing different versions of the product, without enough experience of the manufacturing problems their designs caused.) Also some people will travel with the product, as it moves through towards production. This ensures that their expertise is passed on to the next stage of the operation while also allowing other people, with different skills, to become involved and to perform the task at which they are expert. Thus at each phase of its development the product is being handled by people with particular experience in that area operating within systems which suit their cultures, tasks and time-frames.

Organizations in the 1990s

Increasingly organizations are going to be forced to rethink their structures. The most common sight in the 1990s will probably be more large bureaucratic-type organizations trying to adapt to a political, economic and social environment where the speed of change continues to accelerate. Two important changes will be that getting new products to the market faster will become the key competitive issue and that there will be a continuing shift away from unskilled workers to skilled and 'knowledge' workers (workers who can operate high technology processes).

Some of the features of organizations which try to adapt will be:

- Flatter structures, with fewer levels of management so they can process information faster and be more responsive to changes in the environment.
- Managers will no longer have the knowledge which their workers possess. So they will move towards becoming 'coordinators' of experts rather than 'controllers' of subordinates.

- There will be greater use of cross-functional teams so that organizations can coordinate activities to occur simultaneously rather than sequentially. This will be aimed at cutting down product development times and dealing with more complex problems which require a combination of different types of expertise.
- Operations will be decentralized to promote more responsibility, participation and commitment from a more highly educated workforce. But certain activities will be centralized to make best use of limited resources, such as expensive facilities or specialized knowledge.
- There will be a shortage of certain key skills, so being able to acquire, develop and retain particular groups of knowledge workers will be essential to an organization's success. This will mean major changes in personnel management, in particular paying people more for their rarity value and contribution rather than for their official position or seniority. Younger experts may start earning as much as or more than older managers.
- Organizations will improve the way they develop and communicate their strategies, as there will be no time to wait and see what competitors are doing and then follow them.

These changes will cause considerable strains in many organizations. Often structure will fall out of line with what the environment dictates. Or else structure and systems will not change at the same speed and will start working against, rather than assisting each other.

A simple, but effective, way of trying to prevent structure, systems and environment falling out of line with each other is to go through the following series of questions once a year.

1. What business are we in?
2. How are we going to compete in that business?
3. What are the factors which are critical to our success in that business?
4. What is our organization's main goal?
5. What are the goals of each major department?
6. Do the departmental goals support or hinder the organization's goal?
7. What are the main measures used for evaluating each department's performance?
8. Do these help or prevent the department contributing to the organization's goals?

If these basic questions are answered honestly they can often reveal a drift towards misalignment of systems, structure and environment, which will need to be corrected if the organization is to be successful.

13
Organizational culture

Every organization has a different feel to it. Some consist of long hushed corridors, closed doors with well-polished brass nameplates, and groups of minions huddled obediently together at regular intervals. Others may pulse with activity – open-plan offices or open office doors, people earnestly discussing, a sense of purpose in the air. Others just look tired – shabby buildings, desks piled high with papers, people moving around with no sense of urgency. This 'feel' is part of what has come to be called the organization's 'culture'. To understand the workings of any organization, it is essential to understand its culture – both why it came about and how it influences people's thoughts and behaviour.

An organization's culture works at many different levels and is intricately bound up with its structure. Culture is formed by a number of different influences – the organization's past, its environment, its systems, the type of people and management it has and so on. Culture can be very strong and permeate every aspect of the organization. Culture can be described as the set of attitudes, values, styles and behaviours of an organization. The amount of freedom allowed to individuals, the levels of energy, the way people communicate, the kinds of people who are successful – all these are part of the organization's culture. Different organizations also have their own myths, heroes, villains, taboo subjects and language. The culture is visible in the way people behave, the way they talk and the surroundings they work in. The organization's culture is the way it views the world and interacts with it. Thus it is critical for an organization to be aware of its own particular culture and to appreciate its strengths and weaknesses.

In an article in 1972 Dr Roger Harrison proposed four main cultural types.[8] Possibly no organization is totally one type and within each organization different departments will display variations on the overall organization's culture. However most organizations will be predominantly one type or the other and the classification provides a useful way of viewing any organization.

Power culture (Autocracy)

Usually found in organizations or departments which have been built up or run by strong charismatic individuals. In the centre is the 'great man' who retains control and around him are his management team – his 'courtiers' and 'courtesans' – who live to serve his wishes. Normally there are few written rules and procedures. If these do exist they are seldom adhered to, because decisions tend to be made on the basis of who has power and influence rather than the logic of formal procedures. It may be exciting and rewarding to be amongst or near to the inner circle of courtiers, but it can also be dangerous as people and groups can quickly fall out of favour – with quite serious consequences for their futures. This culture tends to attract people who like risk and political infighting and can survive in a turbulent environment where contacts, influence and possession of information are crucial to success.

Strengths

Power cultures tend to be tough, aggressive and self-confident. They are not slowed down by committees and procedures, so can react quickly to threats or opportunities. Often they thrive on change and look for new ventures to become involved in. They can be challenging and exhilarating to work in.

Weaknesses

They can be very dependent on the great man. If he loses touch with the environment, his judgement fails or he grows weak, they may still carry out his bidding, however inappropriate. Rapid growth can put strains on the central figure and distract him from what he is good at. If he dies, there can be a sudden power vacuum and succession problems, unless he has thought through and prepared for his departure. If there are problems, a power culture may be unaware of the need to react to them, as nobody dares be the bringer of bad news. Also they can become too involved with political infighting as executives jostle for position. One commentator talked of the inner circle of courtiers as being 'gentlemen with stilettos' and of 'not knowing your throat had been cut till you nodded your head in agreement and it fell off'.

Role culture (Bureaucracy)

These are often larger organizations with clearly defined structures, roles and procedures. They are most people's idea of a bureaucracy. Individual people and their abilities are much less important than their roles in the structure. These roles and the way they interrelate are fixed as if engraved in stone and people are chosen not for their spread of abilities but for how well they will fit a particular role. They offer a secure, stable environment, where each person knows precisely what is expected of him and any performance in excess of this may be seen as disruptive. Communication tends to be either written or through regular meetings of committees and steering groups. The most obvious role cultures are government departments, banks, insurance companies and the finance and administration sections of major organizations. Growth often pushes the other three cultures towards a role culture, as the need to control a large organization calls for standardization and centralization of power.

Strengths

Role cultures are normally successful when the external environment is stable and the main task is simple and repetitive. They are good at the efficient allocation and control of resources, achieving economies of scale. They can provide safety and predictability for their members, which may even extend to lifetime employment. In return they ask for limited ambition and full obedience to their codes of practice.

Weaknesses

They can be slow to perceive the need for change, usually see change as a threat and are often unable to adapt to it. While they thrive in a stable environment, or one they control, a sudden shock like deregulation or a new technology can leave them floundering. Either they decline and disappear or are forced to go through rapid and traumatic change, frequently involving the replacement of senior management. When times become difficult, they tend to resort to tried and tested ways of operating rather than finding new ways to be successful. Their inflexibility means they are weak at innovation and creative, ambitious or imaginative people will become frustrated and leave. The main challenge for these bureaucratic organizations over the next ten years will be how to maintain their formal, hierarchical structures, while at the same time creating 'islands of innovation' – areas free of restrictive control, where new products and services can be quickly developed.

Task culture (Adhocracy)

This kind of organization is focused on the need to accomplish certain tasks or projects. It will bring together people from different functions and with differing areas of expertise to work in ad hoc teams on specific projects. When the task is completed the people will then be assigned to other projects. Influence is widely dispersed and power tends to go to those with certain skills rather than to those who hold formal positions. In fact, although people may clearly have different official titles, these are often sacrificed to the needs of each project team. Teams, and individuals in teams, have a high degree of independence in how they work as long as they are achieving results. Control is exercised by the centre through how projects are allocated and also regular project audits. Lateral relationships with colleagues are key to success (rather than vertical relationships as in a role culture). In the 1960s and 1970s task cultures were seen by behavioural scientists as 'the way' forward, because they appeared to offer democracy, participation, job satisfaction and the opportunities for the individual to develop his potential.

Strengths

They are quick to adapt to change and good at innovation. They tend to value their employees as individuals and to invest in them by developing their knowledge and skills. They have few levels of management, loose structures and fit in well with modern ideas of equality and individual freedom.

Weaknesses

They can be difficult to control and are often very wasteful with money and other resources. Their members see any attempt to control their profligacy as bureaucratic interference and will often leave rather than submit to more formal financial accountability. They function well during times of growth, but in difficult conditions they can degenerate into political infighting over allocation of projects and resources.

Person culture (Democracy)

This is more of a theoretical ideal which is seldom found in reality. But many organizations are influenced by it and have tried to move closer to it. In a person culture, the organization exists for the benefit of the individuals working in it, rather than vice versa. Because they are free to develop and use their own knowledge and talents, they can make a much greater contribution than people who feel controlled by an organization. There is no formal structure. Instead there is a group of 'experts' who join together to share facilities and experience. Hospital consultants, some law practices, small media production companies, some R & D departments and some families function in a manner resembling a person culture. The trend in many organizations is to try and reproduce, as far as possible, the conditions of this culture, as it is felt it encourages loyalty, productivity and creativity through aiming at employee satisfaction.

Strengths

This is the kind of atmosphere most people would prefer to work in. It is believed to be the most dynamic and innovatory and is not seen as exerting coercive pressure on its members.

Weaknesses

The more an organization grows the greater are the pressures towards developing formal structures, controls and hierarchies. Person cultures are usually only possible in very small groups. Frequently dominant personalities will upset the balance of power, causing dissatisfaction and friction. Also, person cultures have difficulties in controlling resources and in being single-minded and competitive.

14
Organizations as political systems

There are three main ways of looking at organizations – as bureaucratic structures where form and procedure determines action, as cultural entities each with its own particular set of beliefs and behaviours, and as political systems in which different factions constantly struggle for power and influence. We are taught that in argument reason wins and so we tend to underestimate the significance of politics in organizational life.

All organizations are made up of different interest groups. These can be formed around a number of axes – functional (sales versus production, marketing versus finance), hierarchical (managers versus supervisors), historical patterning (newcomers versus the old guard) or size (small departments versus large departments). Issues of the day may also serve as a focus of conflict – should the organization grow, remain stable or contract, should they invest in new technology or not, should they expand abroad or not? Management control systems may exacerbate political differences by giving conflicting goals to departments who are meant to be cooperating. If sales are being judged (and rewarded) on the basis of total volume sold (irrespective of profitability), production are aiming at making the optimum volume at the lowest cost (without too much expensive overtime or subcontracting) and finance are interested in profitability, the stage is set for a battle which can never be resolved to everybody's satisfaction. In addition different groups may have different goals, time-orientations, values, styles of behaviour, techniques of problem-solving, even languages – all of which can lead to poor communication, conflict and political activity.

In summary, organizations consist of different groups with differing rationales and there will be continual competition for power and influence between them. Political behaviour can be seen as the behaviour of interest groups and individuals as they compete for scarce resources such as budgets, people, tasks, territory, status, power and technology. In times of expansion political activity tends to reduce as interest groups see their demands being satisfied. Therefore other groups do not appear to be a threat. But in stagnation or retraction, political activity will increase as groups become aware of the limits on available resources and believe they can only achieve their own goals at the expense of other groups.

Political activity and change

Change is probably one of the major catalysts to political activity. Change, by definition, means that the distribution of resources may be unscrambled and some new pattern arrived at. Each group will fight to defend its current allocation or even for an increase and this struggle will lead to a great release of political energy, often at the expense of the organization's overall effectiveness. Change will often divide an organization into four main factions: those who held power previously, who may feel threatened and will be inclined to resist change, those who believe in the need for change, those who don't care either way, and those who felt dispossessed before and will support the change in the hope of receiving more than they had previously.

Dynamic conservatism

One way in which political activity can lead to an organization becoming misaligned with its environment, and ultimately to the failure of that organization, has been called 'dynamic conservatism'. The name stems from the fact that the forces which strive to maintain the status quo become active and succeed in strengthening their position at the expense of the organization's ability to adapt.

The process of 'dynamic conservatism' can briefly be described as follows:

1. In a time of stability the most powerful and conservative groups manage to gain the greatest amount of resources, power and influence as their methods are seen to be successful. They are also first to acquire any new resources because of their strong position.
2. The environment changes. The weakest groups are usually those who will first notice the change, as they are the most vulnerable and therefore the most ready to adapt.
3. The weaker groups announce the change in the environment. This is seen as a threat by the powerful groups and so is dismissed.
4. The change in the environment gradually becomes impossible to ignore. The organization begins to adjust. The least powerful are the first to lose resources and in general lose most.
5. The organization emerges from the shock with the powerful conservative forces having made the smallest sacrifice. The organization is possibly now even more conservative than before and is less able to adapt to the next change in the environment.

It is in this way that the central administration areas of some organizations seem to survive every shock, while other (more productive) departments always appear to lose out. Finally so little is left to support the large central administration that performance sinks to an unacceptable level. Dramatic and powerful action, usually by someone brought in from outside, then cuts away much of the unproductive central core and thus reverses the process of dynamic conservatism.

Dealing with politics

There is a tendency in organizations only to deal with politics when they exceed certain acceptable levels – for example when they lead to open conflict. This fire-fighting approach will normally only smooth over any local flare-up and does little to solve the underlying issues. While politics will never be removed from an organization, there are ways of harnessing political energy into more positive channels.

The most basic step is to develop an overall organization strategy that is realistic, provides some degree of challenge (organizational stretch), is simple and comprehensible and is well and repeatedly communicated down through the organization. This may be increasing market share by 20 per cent over two years, becoming the cheapest producer, providing the best customer service measured in number of repeat visits or shortest throughput times, or whatever. But it has to be something everyone in the organization can understand and identify with. Strategies like 'increasing the dividend paid to shareholders by 10 per cent' are hardly likely to capture the enthusiasm and interest of the members, unless they themselves are shareholders. Strategy must provide a superordinate goal for all groups to aim at.

Each department or area should then develop its own strategy as to how it will contribute towards achieving the overall organization strategy. There is no point having a personnel policy which is well-meaning but not geared to overall organizational goals, or a capital investment plan which will do wonders for the production manager's status, but happens to be out of line with what the organization is trying to accomplish.

Individual departments should measure their performance and implement reward systems based on how well they are achieving the company's strategic objectives. For example, if the goal is maximizing short-term profit, sales reps should be paid bonus on the profitability of sales, not just the total volume sold. Or if you are trying to improve customer service by making smaller batches more frequently, you do not judge and reward production on the basis of total output. Or if you are trying to create a dynamic research and development team then you could start to measure personnel on how many people stay with the company and what percentage of graduates leave for better jobs within their first five years.

Above all, you try to create a situation where people channel their energies into achieving one or two common goals, instead of pursuing departmental or sectional interests at the expense of the organization.

15
Power in organizations

For some people, power is a dirty word. It implies one person controlling another, manipulation and loss of freedom. Yet it is an obvious reality of organizational life that the use of power is at least as important as the structure and culture of the organization in determining what decisions are made. The concept of power does not need to be negative, though usually it is seen as such.

Power is used by people in an organization to achieve certain effects based on their perception of the organization's or their own interests. Power itself can be manipulated as people's perceptions, which lie behind their use of power, are open to influence. There are many sources of power and different styles of power will be more or less successful depending on the nature of the organization. Power is a relational concept; it cannot exist in a vacuum. It depends on, at least, two people – the person who uses it and the person at whom it is directed. An individual's use of power is a function of his awareness of its existence, possession, skill at control, tactical abilities and personality (courage, ambition, willingness to use power, morality). Its effectiveness will also be a function of its target's belief in it or vulnerability to it – for example, too often superiors threaten sanctions which subordinates know will never be realized or offer rewards which people don't think are worth the effort acquiring. Or else a manager may use one power source so overtly or so often that people resent it and react against it.

Power will be most successful when it is believed to be used in an open and legitimate way, it is carefully targeted and is applied maturely in the company's interest rather than to further individual ambition. Misused or badly thought-out use of power will tend to rebound on the user.

Sources of power

Awareness

Some managers are unsuccessful in certain actions because they do not realize the variety of power sources available to them. Technical experts often believe that logic backed up by endless detail will convince their audience. Experienced organizational politicians may rely too heavily on their manipulative skills. Department heads will assume that their authority alone is sufficient to cause their subordinates to act in a certain way. Most situations require the use of a combination of power sources and the manager who is most aware of these has an advantage over the person who has a more limited range.

Resource and reward

This is based on the ability to offer rewards (promotion, pay rises, extra resources) or to punish. The rewards and sanctions may be tangible such as more pay or delayed promotion or they may be more intangible, for example friendship, respect, inclusion into certain groups, acceptance. In very bureaucratic organizations this tends to be limited by official rules and procedures, whereas in looser organizations it may be one of the most effective power sources.

Position

Occupying a certain official position in the organizational hierarchy can give clear authority over others. Positional power may allow you to directly decide what subordinates do. Or else you may be able to influence them by influencing the environment in which people work – setting priorities, designing jobs, delegating – what is called 'managing the ecology'. Position power can also work in more subtle ways. It may give you access to certain information, which rivals or subordinates may not possess. Or it may allow you into various networks, meetings or groups where you can come into contact with the key figures in an organization.

Expertise

In some situations being the acknowledged expert may give you considerable power to influence decision-making. This source of power is less resented than some others, but it is also vulnerable. If the expert is seen to have been wrong, he will find it hard to regain credibility. Moreover he is only expert until a greater expert appears, then he loses most of his power. Expert power is more effective in task cultures than in role cultures or highly political environments. The strength of expert power tends to be overestimated by experts and they can be surprised when political, personal or other considerations take preference over their expertise.

Traditions, norms and processes

Understanding the traditions, norms and processes of an organization can be a considerable source of power. Either you can use the rules and procedures to circumscribe the freedom of others or else you can advertise your loyalty to the organization's values and clothe self-interest in an aura of being synonymous with the organization's overall goals. Also you can 'manage meaning' – if in a position of authority you may be able to change the overall organization's goals, which would immediately strengthen the hand of your supporters and weaken the opposition. For example, moving focus from production to marketing, from long-term survival to short-term profitability, or from customer service to meeting financial goals can dramatically alter the balance of power in an organization.

Personal

Many people have individual characteristics – charisma, personality, dynamism – which make others want to be near them, listen to their opinions and do what they suggest. This can either reinforce the other power sources or else be a means of working around them. There is a tendency for managers to attribute their success to personal power, when much of it is in fact due to position power. The managing director or headmaster who moves aside to allow his successor to take over can appear like King Lear handing his kingdom over to his daughters. He is surprised when he is no longer consulted, respected and obeyed, because he had not realized that much of his former power had come from his position rather than his person.

Negative

This source of power is possessed both by managers and subordinates. It is the power to prevent things happening, to delay actions or information, to distort communication. This is most often used by 'gate-keepers' – these are people

Some managers have difficulty making key decisions

who have the power to decide what information reaches other people or who is permitted access to influential figures. Secretaries, personal assistants, senior management groups all are in a position where they can filter information and screen people, so the key decision-maker has a particular view of reality.

Information

Information can give power at several levels. There is the ability to process, analyse and draw useful conclusions and the ability to consolidate and present information in a convincing way. Access to certain information can be the key to being aware of what behaviours, proposals and actions are likely to meet with approval or success. Also the ability to control the flow of information both up and down through an organization can give a manager many advantages.

Reduction of uncertainty

In situations where there is a great deal of uncertainty about what course of action to follow, a person can take charge by being willing to act when others are wavering. The person does not need to know the answer – the fact that he is prepared to show leadership is usually sufficient. Then later, when the others have rallied behind him, he can use them as resources for discovering the best way forward. Faced by a high degree of uncertainty some people are willing to sacrifice their freedom to the person who appears able to reduce that uncertainty.

Self-interest

Considerable power can be gained by persuading people that you both share the same goals or that it would be in their self-interest to cooperate with you. If you can bring them round to identifying with your cause, then you may have created a willing accomplice, who becomes more and more linked to you and may find it very difficult later to try and switch loyalties.

MANAGING CHANGE

16 Change and resistance

17 Sensing the problem

18 Starting the change process

19 Managing the change process

20 Common responses to the need for change

16
Change and resistance

Many experts would have us believe that we are living through a time of more rapid change compared to any period in the past. Yet anyone who has experienced either of the World Wars or the Great Depression might feel that the last thirty years have been a period of unrivalled stability and prosperity. What has probably happened is that the nature of change itself has changed. Up until the 1950s change was mostly linked to major, even cataclysmic, political events, to which people were forced to adapt. In the last twenty to thirty years, changes have been mainly social, technological and commercial – the growth of an educated work force with high aspirations, the rapid pace of technological development mostly linked to electronics, and the increase and globalization of competition. And each organization has had to find its own response.

The reason why the problem of organizational change has become so topical may be linked to two main factors. Firstly, environmental change seems to have become a continuous and accelerating process. And secondly, due to their higher education and expectations people can no longer be ordered to adapt, and so successful management of the human element has become a much more crucial part of the effective implementation of change.

Content and process

One way of looking at change is to divide it into 'content' and 'process'. 'Content' refers to the more tangible elements which are to be changed, the 'what' of a change programme – systems, machinery, responsibilities, structure. 'Process' is the 'how', the way in which the actual changes will be carried out. In the West, we tend to be quite successful at defining the content, but have more problems with the process – the human element of change. It is difficult obtaining figures on failed attempts at change as few organizations want their weaknesses exposed. But one study showed that 70 per cent of British companies which invested in automation were disappointed with the results. While another indicated that the productivity of advanced technology in European manufacturing was between 20 and 50 per cent (depending on the country) less productive than in Japan.

Organizations in the West have a natural tendency to remain in equilibrium. They prefer and function best in conditions of stability. Yet if we now believe that continuous change is to become a permanent feature of organizational life, we need to learn ways of implementing change quickly and constructively for an organization to survive. We have to become better at the process of change. The number of once great organizations who have diminished or disappeared in the last twenty years – the European steel, camera, motorbike industries or the American nuclear industry for example – shows the importance of being able to adapt to changing environmental conditions.

Resistance to change

People resist change. Every manager knows that. It is as if people are stupid and managers and organizations are not. Yet many managers also often resist change. The fact is that often what people do resist is not change itself, but the way it is introduced. The content may be acceptable, but if the process is mishandled, the forces of resistance will come into play.

If we use the model of people acting on three levels – rational, emotional and political – we can try and analyse some of the reasons resistance to change occurs.

Rational

- They believe the change to be wrong, the time to be wrong or the methods inappropriate.
- They don't feel their views or the views of their section have been taken into account.
- They have seen other management decisions miss the mark and view this as just one more.
- They do not believe management/the organization have the ability to successfully implement the change.
- They see no benefit in it for themselves.

Emotional

- Change means criticism of the way things are done at the moment, criticism of them. They may even be responsible for building up current systems.
- Management have broken their promises in the past, so there is a low level of trust now. People believe there is some hidden agenda behind management's desire to change (for example, reducing the number of staff).
- They are afraid of not being able to cope with the changes, of looking stupid or failing in the new environment.
- They have low tolerance for ambiguity and prefer stability to turbulence.
- They don't understand the reasons and implications of the change and feel general anxiety because they don't know how it will operate in practice.

Political

- They think they will lose power, status, authority, freedom.
- They believe the skills they have will become less important, even that they may lose their jobs.
- There is pressure on them from colleagues to resist.

Thus resistance to change does not necessarily stem from people's stupidity. It can come from a range of rational and irrational sources and is often rooted deep in people's feelings and beliefs. It is therefore critical that leaders of an organization invest time and energy in the process of change as well as the content. Most changes in organizations are not pushing back the frontiers of science, rather they are taking techniques and/or technologies which have been proven elsewhere. Thus most failure in implementing change must come from the human aspect of change rather than the technical.

Models of change

There are many theoretical models of how change should be introduced. These range from those which propose that there are three or four clear, sequential steps to those which see the process as much more complex. There are so many factors that influence the way change should be implemented – the degree of change, the level of trust between management and staff, the urgency of change, the openness of the organization to change, the personalities of key managers – that it may be misleading to suggest any particular model as being the best.

Instead, the sections on Managing Change will give examples of a number of different aspects of each stage of implementing change, which may be more or less useful, depending on the situation any manager finds himself in.

Positive and negative attitudes

One feature common to all organization changes is the importance of management's attitude to the change process. If management view the task as 'overcoming resistance to change' or 'driving change through' or even 'knocking the organization into shape', it may give them a pleasing image of themselves as 'macho-managers'. But it also means they already have a negative attitude. They see people and the organization as something to be pushed, bullied, browbeaten or manipulated against its will. And this negative orientation will show itself in the way they plan changes and how they treat people. Usually it will also become a self-fulfilling prophecy – if you believe people will resist, you are not open and trusting with them. They will sense the lack of openness and trust, feel information is being withheld and react with hostility. Management's expectation of resistance thus becomes reality (and incidentally management's belief in people being inherently stubborn or stupid is confirmed).

However, management can try and adopt a more positive viewpoint where they are 'helping to coordinate change' or even 'unleashing the potential of the people in the organization to improve its performance'. Then they see themselves as resources rather than controllers. This will lead to them having a more positive attitude to people and the process, which may create a positive self-fulfilling prophecy. People will now be invited to contribute to the change implementation, rather than being pushed into resisting it.

Managers welcome the challenge of implementing change

17
Sensing the problem

The major issue at the start of any change process is not so much 'how to achieve a certain change' but 'how to open up the organization to the possibility of change'. Many managements have failed in change efforts because they have tried to follow the problem with the solution. Managers can become too enthusiastic at finding 'the solution' and attempt to impose it on an organization which has not yet seen any need for change. The first stage in any change is to try to take the whole organization through a learning process, so that awareness of the mismatch between the organization and its environment is spread down to all levels.

Unfreezing, moving, freezing

One model of implementing change suggests that you first need to 'unfreeze' the organization, by educating it about the need for change. Once this general understanding of the problem has been created, resistance to change will be reduced as people perceive the necessity and have probably already begun thinking about and discussing solutions. Then you can start to 'move' the organization to the desired state. Once that is achieved you should 'freeze' the organization in its new state.

Other models propose that an organization should not be frozen again, but that you need to create an environment where it is permanently adapting to change. However the key point is that until knowledge of the need for change is widely and repetitively communicated, resistance will be high.

Developing concern

Concern over a mismatch between an organization and its environment should not just be management's problem. It should be communicated down through the organization so that it becomes everyone's property. One theory talks of orchestrating concern so it becomes part of everyone's agenda. If there is a need to become less product and more market-oriented, or to control costs, or to improve customer service, by giving the problem to everybody you can already start discussion of solutions both formally in meetings and informally. Instead of people using their energy to resist change, they can be encouraged to employ it positively in assisting the change process.

Doomsday scenario

One way of focusing people on the need for change is to ask the question 'what happens if we do nothing'. By creating a 'doomsday scenario' where the organization stands still while the environment continues to move, you highlight the necessity for action. Otherwise people may pay lip service to the need for change without really believing in it.

Constructing a crisis

If there is a need for a major organizational change, management can make the message dramatically clear by 'constructing a crisis'. In preparing their annual results, companies have considerable leeway in deciding how much profit or loss to declare by adopting different accounting procedures. One major European company, who had never before made a loss, chose deliberately to announce a loss one year in order to show all the employees unambiguously that the time had come for a significant change in the way they operated.[9]

Compliance, identification, internalization

A way of understanding the importance of all the people in an organization sensing the problem is to consider the three levels at which people can respond to a request from management.

1. Compliance is doing something because you have been told to rather than because you believe it is necessary.
2. Identification is where a person sees the need to act in a certain way, even though he may not want to.
3. Internalization occurs when a person changes behaviour because he both sees the need and wants to, as he finds it fits in with his beliefs.

Changes which result from compliance seldom last, because people will eventually fall back to the behaviours they believe to be right. Successful change requires at least identification and ideally internalization. By making the decision to invest the time and energy in having people sense and own the problem, you move towards making the change process something that is believed in rather than complied with.

18
Starting the change process

Defining the desired end state

A useful early step in the change process is to try and make a detailed description of the desired end state and to communicate this to all the people who will be affected. Doing this brings a number of benefits.

- People's anxieties are reduced because they can visualize what will happen and so feel less uncertainty.
- The organization has a clear target to aim at.
- Working towards a shared vision is a constructive activity, one that generates optimism. Many change programmes which have no such vision take place in an atmosphere of hostility, failure and pessimism.
- People are given something to build on and can begin to see roles for themselves in both the change process and the desired end state.
- If management have made some wrong assumptions, it allows people the chance to identify these and try to correct them.

It is not easy to prescribe how detailed the description of the desired end state should be. It should be detailed enough for people to be able to start thinking constructively about it. Statements like 'we must improve customer service to be better than our competitors' or 'we will reduce the number of rejects by 30 per cent' are obviously inadequate as they say nothing about what actions or changes will achieve the goal. Saying 'rejects will be reduced by giving operators the responsibility for quality control, implementing statistical quality control procedures, running cross-functional quality circles, changing the payment system to increase the influence quality has on salaries, and starting a programme to analyse key machine tolerances' at least gives some picture of how people will be affected. On the other hand a too detailed description of the end state may run the risk of appearing set in stone and not giving people the chance to give their input and see it influencing the outcome.

Defining the current state

As part of making people aware of the need for change, management may need to provide a realistic assessment of how things currently stand. This may include a description of the strengths and weaknesses of the existing methods of operating and a comparison of the current situation with the desired state in order to highlight those areas which must change. This should not be too negative, otherwise people may feel criticized and disheartened. For example, often when new management take over, they tend to paint a fairly black picture of conditions, both to try and shock people out of their apathy and to create a situation where even the most modest improvement will leave them looking like heroes. This can backfire by turning the organization against them and causing people to take delight, consciously or subconsciously, in any setbacks the new management meets.

Perhaps the main advantage of communicating a clear description of the current state is that it gives everyone a common base to work from. As long as people have significantly different opinions of the present effectiveness of the organization, then they will not be able to agree about the actions to be taken or their necessity.

Planning change

The change plan is clearly concerned with how to move from the generally accepted current state to the desired end state. Like all plans this should include a communication schedule (who will be told what when and how often), an activity schedule (what must be done, by whom, within what time-frame) and measurable goals so that success, or otherwise, can be objectively assessed.

A comprehensive plan will try and address how change will be achieved at three levels:

1. Formal technical systems – what changes will there be in equipment, systems, technology and operating procedures?
2. Formal structures – who will be responsible for what, what will be their official position, who will report to whom and what will be the changes in status or rewards?
3. Informal structures – where are the main power or interest groups and how will they be affected?

A key part of the plan will be an identification of:

- Who will be the winners in the process and how can they be used to help implement the changes?
- Who will be the losers (of power, authority, status, respect), how will they resist the changes, what can they be offered to lower their opposition?
- Who might, mistakenly, believe they will be a loser because they have received inadequate information, how can communication be improved to ensure they do not misunderstand the situation and oppose the changes?

Choice of transition manager

In any but the most minor change you will probably need to appoint one person as being responsible for managing the change process. The importance of this position tends to be underestimated and the choice of the wrong person can sink the whole programme.

If the person is responsible for the current situation and plays a key role in the way things operate, he is unlikely to really believe in the need for change. He will tend to look for problems rather than solutions, to view difficulties as proof that things were better as they were, and will not be concerned by delays. In general, he may have little real interest in the success of the process and will not be able to generate the enthusiasm and confidence which will be necessary to motivate others.

Choosing the sponsor of the new methods as transition manager also has its dangers. He may be too eager to see his brainchild up and running and bulldoze his ideas through without considering even legitimate criticism. The result may then be a system which is inappropriate or ineffective. Also he may be too keen to throw out existing methods, both good and bad.

One solution can be to have these two people jointly responsible. But most frequently, unless they are exceptional people, this will lead to conflict and political infighting with each busily building up support for his position.

The most successful choice is normally someone who has no deep vested interest either in the current or future state. His lack of technical knowledge in the area will be more than made up for by his ability to take a reasonably objective view. It is generally accepted that a transition manager should have three main characteristics:

1. the authority to drive through the change if discussion and negotiation fail to overcome resistance;
2. the power to obtain sufficient resources to carry out the change when there will be conflicting demands on resources from those responsible for maintaining normal operations while the change is under way;
3. considerable interpersonal skills including the ability to negotiate, to obtain respect, to generate enthusiasm and to sell ideas.

Choice of management style

Change is seldom carried out at an organization's leisure. While things are going well few organizations have the foresight to plan for harder times. Change normally only occurs when the mismatch with the environment is so great that change is finally recognized to be unavoidable. Change thus will tend to happen under considerable pressure and this may push an organization towards adopting a much more autocratic approach than it knows it should.

To underline the importance of resisting the pressure to force change through in the shortest possible time, it might be worth briefly describing an exaggerated, but not uncommon, management attitude.

'Management knows best'

Only management know what is right for the organization. This concerns both major strategic decisions and detailed operating matters. Therefore we will have to drag the organization into the future. We should lay down the law, be suspicious of any ideas subordinates may have, see any resistance as due to unwillingness to change rather than legitimate concerns over new methods and stick rigidly to our original change plan whatever objections people in the organization may raise.

Needless to say, such an approach may generate compliance, but it will not lead to successful, lasting change.

Participation to coercion

Any change situation will necessarily be confrontational. The more people can be encouraged to participate in the change, the more confrontation can be avoided and political energy channelled into positive action rather than into negative resistance. Normally management will have to adopt various styles depending on the reasons for and level of resistance. The list below suggests six styles ranging from participative to coercive. It may be useful for managers to think through whether they have made sufficient effort to use the first three styles before they move to the latter three.

Education and communication: lets people understand why change is necessary; produces a shared diagnosis of the problem; encourages positive support.

Participation and involvement: people become part of, not victims of, the change process; they feel that they have ownership of the changes and will work to ensure they are successful.

Helping and support: the target group is willing to move but lacks either the confidence or the ability; management provides advice and resources.

Negotiation and agreement: some part of the organization will lose out and has the power to resist; they may have to be bought out, bribed with the offer of power or resources if they will stop opposing change

Manipulation: management gives out carefully chosen information to suggest to resisters that they have much to gain from complying, while downplaying any negatives; people who resist are offered benefits in return for cooperation.

Open or implicit coercion: speed is essential and there is no time for further discussion; people are given to understand that failure to cooperate will lead to some form of sanctions.

19
Managing the change process

Building on success

Any change programme will be at its most vulnerable around the half-way point. By this time the investment has been made, coordinating groups set up, action been taken. Yet probably there will be few, if any, results. People may start to become disheartened and wonder if all the work was worth while. Those who were always opposed will often choose this moment to attack and the evidence – a lot of effort for little outcome – will put them in a strong position. The situation begins to look bleak, political activity increases and optimism turns to pessimism.

Managers should not be caught out by this. They should instead take action to prevent it affecting the programme. For example, they can prepare their subordinates for this stage and cooperate with them to work out ways of coming through it. Also they should aim at achieving some small, early and easily demonstrable successes. These should then be broadcast as encouragement to take people over the pessimism of this period. It can be dangerous to approach change on too broad a front. A better approach may be to split it into smaller, more easily manageable units so that early success can lead to increased motivation.

Force-field analysis

This is one of the more powerful tools for helping to plan change strategy. The theory is that in any change situation there are 'driving' and 'restraining' forces. The driving forces are those which favour the change, the restraining forces are those which oppose it. Force-field analysis is designed to give a clearer view of what the driving and restraining forces are and their relative strengths. The figure opposite shows a simplified force field based on a proposal for two European companies who are competitors in a market to enter into a collaborative agreement, in order to prevent the Japanese taking over this market.

By identifying the two sets of forces and their relative strengths a manager can develop a logical strategy for dealing with the forces opposing change. Some people believe that it is better to start with the strongest restraining force, as once this is neutralized the weaker ones will start to crumble. Others suggest that you should begin with the weaker restraining forces as here you have more chance of early success. But there is general agreement that strengthening the driving

Driving forces

Restraining forces

Fear of Japanese

History of rivalry and distrust between firms

New director's policy

Opposition from senior management group

Need to exchange technology to improve products

R & D fear their role will diminish

1992 removal of trade barriers

Belief in customers' loyalty

Support from younger middle management

Organization's fear of change

Present status quo

(The longer the line, the stronger the force)

Figure 5

forces will often just lead to a stiffening of the restraining forces. So you have to have a clear plan for reducing the restraining forces if you are to be successful.

Change implementation

There are a number of actions which can assist in implementing a change programme:

Objective

The process should have a clear realistic objective and not a multiplicity of aims. If there are too many goals, people may disagree over priorities or lose focus.

Message

The message of the need for change should be clear, easily comprehensible and repeated often. People must understand that it is not a transient management whim to be ignored till management think up some other fashionable new idea. They have to realize that the change process will happen because management is serious this time. The message must emanate from the top, be obviously supported by the top and also be seen to be believed in throughout the management hierarchy. If an influential figure is openly disagreeing with the policy, it is unlikely to succeed. Influential people must thus be brought on board, neutralized or moved.

Splitting policy and implementation

The person responsible for the change policy should not also be responsible for the implementation. During the implementation many objections to methods will be raised and adjustments made. If the same person is in charge of policy and implementation, the objections can appear as attacks on the policy itself and adjustments as adjustments to the policy. The credibility of the policy is then weakened. If the two responsibilities are split, people will clearly see that while the details of the implementation plan may be open to debate, the general thrust of the policy is a separate issue and is not up for discussion.

Counter-cultural behaviour

An effective way of signalling change is on the way is for management to take some action which is completely out of keeping with the way things are normally done. This could be having a special room with a flip-chart in it where anyone can anonymously write any suggestion or grievance, top management holding meetings with shop-floor workers, scrapping executive dining rooms to have everyone eat in the same canteen, inviting union representatives to all major management meetings, taking workers, supervisors or quality inspectors out to meet customers, inviting customers to come and meet supervisors to discuss any problems and so on.

Adapting reward systems

Too often change programmes are handicapped by the fact that the reward systems are not changed in line with policy and so actively work against the required new behaviours. For example, a company could not attract promising young graduates to a new electronics division because the group pay scheme was based mainly on length of service – so the company could not offer competitive salaries. Possibly the most common example of this problem is companies trying to improve quality while the pay scheme rewards shop-floor workers for total output. Very often managers overlook the fact that reward systems must be changed to support the types of behaviour management want.

Change agents

Change should not only be driven from the top. Management should try and have change agents at every level in the organization. These could, for example, be members of a change task force. These change agents should meet regularly to discuss their successes and problems. An esprit de corps should be built amongst the change agents to help maintain their cohesion and drive in the face of opposition.

Role models

People who exhibit the required new behaviour should be seen to be encouraged by management. They can then act as role models for others who are hesitant about whether and how to change.

Heretics and deviants

Throughout a change process top management both have to clearly lead the change and yet at the same time maintain operative status – 'mind the shop'.

One device is to use 'heretics' and 'deviants' to say the unsayable – to broadcast the change message. These could range from bringing in an outside consultant, to setting up a special committee to report back on some highly sensitive subject, to commissioning market research which is critical of the company. The key point is that some other source can be used to announce the painful fact that change is necessary.

Creating new arenas

Organizations will tend to deal with new problems in existing ways using existing concepts and behaviours. This may lead to the wrong type of solutions being found. There may be a need to create new arenas where problems can be discussed and resolved. These may be new cross-functional teams, or new department committees or some variation on quality circles. What is important is that by bringing a different group together you will have people see the problems in a different light and break down the old, restrictive patterns of behaviour.

Changing people and portfolios

One way of releasing energy and space for change is to move people and responsibilities. New task forces or teams can be created or new positions established. Managers can be given different roles, which force them to see the situation from a wider perspective than their previous narrow departmental position. Different management groups can meet with different frequencies and deal with different issues from those they are used to. All this can help break down existing routines and also reinforce the message that change is now a reality.

20
Common responses to the need for change

Good times and bad times

A critical issue for most organizations has become the rate and intensity of environmentally-driven change and how the organization adapts to it. A probably over-simplified but useful way of classifying an organization's environment is to talk of 'good times' and 'bad times'.

In 'good times' the mood is one of abundance, expansion and growth. The environment is favourable, policies seem to meet with success and there is little need to worry about controlling resources or arguing about priorities. There is usually little political activity or conflict between groups within the organization as there are plenty of opportunities and resources to satisfy most people's aspirations. The risk is that organizations become blinded by their own success and assume that continued growth will be their natural state.

Not all managers are good at facing facts

In 'good times' other organizations seeing the profits to be had often come rushing into the sector experiencing growth, and create conditions of over-capacity. When the growth bubble bursts, the level of pain can be great, especially to the most recent arrivals, who have made large investments, but not had time to reap the benefits.

When 'bad times' arrive the rallying cry becomes *survival* not *growth*, the individual's concern is keeping his job rather than promotion. Expansion is replaced by talk of control and cutbacks. And political activity increases as departments have to justify their existence and ward off attacks on their resources.

In the West, there appears to be a tendency for organizations to swing between good time and the bad times and to be surprised each time the environment changes. Our individualistic, short-term outlook seems to prevent us from planning ahead and preparing ourselves for the next phase. Listed below are some common wrong responses to changes in the environment.

Ignore/Discount

Changes in the environment are seen as only temporary phenomena and the organization assumes that by weathering the storm everything will come right in the end. An example of this was the lack of response by American car manufacturers to the first oil crisis in the 1970s. This reaction can be due to the whole organization really believing that it is somehow invulnerable. Or else it can be a result of a political process, where the weaker groups in an organization see the need for change and broadcast it. But the strong groups, with a vested interest in the status quo, see the announcement as an attack on their power base rather than an economic reality. They therefore fight to defend their position.

Dynamic conservatism

This has been called 'do as before but more'. In this case the organization does react, but not in a constructive positive way. Here the main power groups, who are responsible for existing policies, tighten their control on the organization, rein in any innovatory activity and bring everything more closely in line with the policies which have been successful in the past. Yet it may be precisely these policies which are now no longer appropriate.

Bad times are only temporary

Possibly the most common response to the arrival of 'bad times'. The organization immediately embarks on a programme of cost-cutting – the work-force is reduced (usually mostly the lower levels), the research budget is slashed, some service functions may be closed down or sold. Management talks of 'belt-tightening' and 'a short period of pain', but there being 'a light at the end of the tunnel'. For a while, management may feel it has ensured the survival of the organization and regained control of the situation. But in fact it has done nothing to deal with the deeper mismatch between the organization's way of operating and its new environment. Finally management may be forced to cut so deeply that they can no longer find any 'fat' to remove. Then either the organization declines and disappears or it is taken over, management replaced and sweeping changes quickly forced through.

Dropping the bomb

Some organizations will only change when the situation has reached crisis proportions. They are unable to build a system which can encourage evolutionary change and so remain static until it is almost too late. Usually it is a new manager who will come and drop the bomb. Coming from outside he can see all the bad attitudes and practices which must be swept away, while existing management are still happy 'rearranging the deck chairs on the Titanic'. Realizing that there is no time for discussion, participation, education, communication and all the other positive methods of causing change, he primes his bomb, comes sweeping in over the terrified employees and unleashes, what appears to the organization to be, destruction and chaos. But by this time it may be the only way of reversing years of stagnation and management neglect.

Executive defence mechanisms

When the 'bad news' arrives, whether it be brought by some bright new manager, a consultant or some other source, there are a number of ways an executive can react. One is to review all the facts objectively and honestly, always thinking what's best for the organization and then to make a balanced, mature decision, not coloured by self-interest or defensiveness. Some other, not always uncommon, ways are suggested below.

Straight rejection: The executive refuses to accept the information presented as relevant or as factual.

Detail hunting: He may say that in principle he agrees or sees that you may have a point. But then he homes in on some minor detail, discusses this at length and allows doubt over some peripheral point to become a stumbling block to his acceptance of the main argument. In Finland these managers are given the colourful epithet of 'point-f***ers'.

Too much to do: He may receive the report but somehow always has too much on his plate to look at it. Or else he may even say he has glanced at the report, it looks very sound and interesting; but he really feels he ought to look at it in a bit more depth before discussing it. Unfortunately he never seems to find the time.

The procedures man: He says he would like to be able to do something, but normal procedure is that such reports are produced by the . . . committee and then passed on to . . . etc.

The emotional tactic: 'How can you do this to me?' might be his reaction, or 'mine isn't the only department with problems', 'I'm doing everything I can!' He tries to use emotion to make you back down.

Already working on it: He thanks you for your input and claims that it only confirms what he already knew. In fact, he already has some people working on precisely that issue, so there's no need to take the matter any further.

But in the future: He says that the time is not quite right at the moment (due to numerous different plausible reasons) for your ideas. But he has no doubt that in the future they will be most helpful.

Generate political support: He sees your ideas as a threat and starts to ring round all his colleagues to express his concerns. As you meet each of them, you find that they all seem to share the first executive's misgivings and your ideas are blocked.

Scapegoat: He would really like to do something, if it wasn't for those idiots in . . . They're the ones who caused the problem and you'll never get them to change.

A committee! He absolutely agrees with your analysis and intends to set up a special committee to look at the problem. This delays the issue till it is forgotten or some new avoidance tactic is employed.

STRATEGY

21 SWOT analysis

22 Portfolio analysis – introduction

23 Portfolio analysis – alternative views

24 Industry structure analysis

25 Supply chain analysis

26 A definition of strategy

27 Managing turnaround

21
SWOT analysis

A SWOT analysis is probably one of the most basic tools for helping to develop strategy. But although it has been accused of being simplistic, it is still a very powerful way for helping an organization (public or private sector) gain a rapid and clear understanding of its environment, on which to start building alternative possible strategies. SWOT is a systematic, rational and disciplined approach, which can assist an organization more from a reactive position, where it always seems to be responding to circumstances, to a proactive stance, where it begins to take control of its destiny. One particular strength of SWOT is that it forces an organization to look not only at its strengths and opportunities, but also at the other side of the coin – its weaknesses and the threats it faces. Very often organizations spend too much time looking for opportunities and too little dealing with the unpleasant business of facing up to those areas where they perform poorly and are vulnerable.

SWOT is short for Strengths, Weaknesses, Opportunities and Threats analysis. The first step in a SWOT is to draw a cross creating four sectors, one each for strengths, weaknesses, opportunities and threats. Then to start listing the current strengths, weaknesses, opportunities and threats facing your organization or department. A sample, simplified SWOT for a medium-sized advertising agency is given in the figure.

SWOTs can be done by individuals. But they can be particularly effective when done by a group, for example the management group of an organization. In a group setting a SWOT can help provide structure, objectivity, clarity and focus to discussions about strategy, which might otherwise tend to wander or else be strongly influenced by personalities and politics.

Checklist

The SWOT should at least cover all of the following areas, each of which may be a source of strengths, weaknesses, opportunities or threats.

Organization's internal features:

- marketing;
- organization structure;
- operations/production;
- finance;

● Experience in retailing sector ● Creative record – awards ● Good at new business presentations ● Reputation of directors	● High level of internal politics ● Little control over expenses ● Low media-buying power (discounts) ● Too many small accounts ● Expensive 'fashionable' location ● No mail order or POS expertise
S	**W**
O	**T**
● Strategic alliance with foreign agencies ● Gain one or two large accounts ● Win more awards ● Grow smaller accounts ● Go after more retail clients ● Develop public service advertising section	● Key personnel leaving (taking clients) ● Downturn in economy ● Profits dependent on biggest two clients ● Growth in specialist creative hot-shops and media-buying specialists ● Clients moving out of capital ● Increase in global advertising

Figure 6 Example (simplified) of a SWOT for a medium-sized advertising agency

- technology;
- human resources;
- management;
- substitute products/services.

Organization's external environment

- macroeconomics;
- politics;
- customers;
- suppliers;
- demographics;
- technology/innovation;
- social trends.

Time and competition

As well as doing a SWOT on an organization's existing situation, there are other SWOTs which can help a manager quickly expand his vision. For example, it may be useful to do a SWOT for an organization, both as the manager sees it now, and as he thinks it might be in one, three, five and even ten years. This can often open up completely new channels of thought and serve as a fertile source of ideas. In addition, it is a simple and effective way for a manager to have other people open their minds and become more receptive to his proposals or concerns.

SWOTs can also be done on main competitors. These may give insights as to what strategy should be adopted or even what strategies they are likely to adopt.

SWOTs can be made for divisions, departments and even individual decisions.

Some difficulties with SWOTs

- SWOTs can tend to reflect a person's existing position and viewpoint. Thus they can be misused to justify a previously decided course of action, rather than being a means of opening up new possibilities.
- Many threats can also be opportunities, depending on a person's attitude. For example, while many companies saw consumers' pressure for environmentally-sound products as a threat, others exploited it, by producing ranges of 'environment-friendly' items.
- SWOTs can allow organizations to take the lazy course of looking for 'fit' rather than 'stretch' – they see what strengths match which opportunities and ignore the opportunities they do not feel they can take advantage of. A more active approach would be to identify the most attractive opportunities and then plan to 'stretch' the organization to meet those opportunities. This would make strategy a challenge to the organization rather than a 'fit' between its existing strengths and the opportunities it chooses to develop.

Choice of strategy

Probably the strongest message from a SWOT analysis is that whatever course of action is decided, it should to some extent contain elements of all of the following – minimizing weaknesses, counteracting threats, building on strengths and seizing opportunities.

Interaction matrix

There is a second step to a SWOT, which is sometimes proposed. This consists of drawing a matrix, then listing either the strengths and weaknesses vertically on the left and threats and opportunities along the top (or else listing the opportunities on the left and strengths horizontally along the top). Then you can give some kind of scoring, depending on whether each strength and weakness will be positively or negatively affected by each opportunity or threat. (A full description is not given here, as we do not believe this adds much to the SWOT analysis.)

An interaction matrix can start to become a laborious process. Also it can take much of the creativity and free-thinking out of a SWOT. It then transforms it into a mathematical exercise, which cannot reflect the richness and multiplicity of the ideas a SWOT can generate.

In summary, a SWOT analysis can be an excellent, rapid tool for exploring the many possibilities in a situation, for looking at competition and into the future, for forcing a systematic approach to both positive and negative features and for communicating ideas, policies and concerns to others.

22
Portfolio analysis – introduction

Background

Portfolio analysis can be described as a methodology for generating a set of strategy options depending on the nature of the markets an organization is in and the organization's specific position within those markets. For example, if a firm is in a strong position in a static market or a weak position in a growing market, the portfolio analysis approach will suggest a number of alternative strategies.

Choosing strategy can be complex when you're under pressure from competitors

Portfolio analysis can be used by a one-product single-unit company as a way of getting a clearer idea of the company's potential. But more generally it is associated with organizations which have a range of products or a number of business units – a portfolio of activities – which compete with each other for investment and other resources. Portfolio analysis helps such an organization build a picture of the relative situations of each of its parts, so it can channel investment to the areas where it will provide the greatest contribution to the organization's future strength. Also, this approach can assist organizations in building a balanced portfolio of businesses, so that sufficient cash is generated to fund investment requirements.

The first portfolio analysis is generally attributed to the Boston Consulting Group. Work which they had done on quantifying the effects of the experience curve highlighted the importance of volume and high market share for achieving cost advantages and improving profitability. In addition, they identified that market share was much easier to gain while a market was growing than when it was static or declining. Market share and market growth were thus used as two scales against which to plot a business unit's position. From that position, a set of strategic options could be developed. There are many different models of portfolio analysis, but they all have a similar format in that they use a matrix with two axes for graphically displaying an organization's portfolio of activities. Portfolio analysis was most widely used during the late 1960s and throughout the 1970s. However, though initially popular, it later raised some controversy and is now much less common.

Boston Consulting Group (BCG) matrix

This classifies products or business units according to two key variables – market growth and market share – and suggests appropriate strategies. These two variables are considered important because:

- In a situation of *market growth* there is increasing future potential and it is easier to gain market share. However, high market growth also usually demands a relatively high level of investment, if the opportunities are to be exploited.
- A strong *market position* generally means a unit will be more profitable due to the effects of the learning curve, and economies of scale in production, distribution, marketing and advertising.

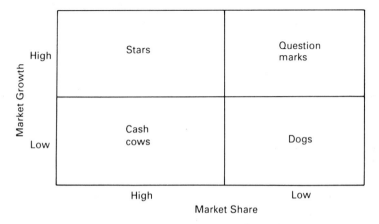

Figure 7 A model of the basic Boston Consulting Group matrix

When plotting products or business units on the matrix, they will fall into one of four quadrants, commonly known as cash cows, stars, question marks and dogs.

Cash cows

Are products which generate large amounts of cash due to their strong market position and yet do not need a lot of cash for investment, as their markets are only growing slowly or else are static or declining. Thus the excess cash they generate can be used to help finance other parts of the business, which may have greater growth potential.

Stars

Have a strong position in growing markets. They may generate some cash, but more often they require more cash than they generate in order to maintain or improve their position. They are generally seen as the future cash cows of the business and so should be given the investment they need, even if they are not profitable in the short term.

Question marks

These are also called 'problem children'. They have low market share in high growth markets. So they will tend to have low profits and weak cash flow, yet be in attractive markets. To strengthen their position and benefit from the market growth, they usually need a high level of investment (well in excess of what they themselves can produce). The question is whether it is worth channelling the resources to a unit which currently has a weak market position. Ideally question marks can be turned into stars with sufficient investment.

Dogs

These either generate little or no cash, as they have a weak position in static markets. Market share can be gained, but as the market is not growing, this can only come from winning custom from competitors and so is likely to be expensive either due to marketing costs or the effects of price reductions.

Choice of strategy

It is generally proposed that there are four basic strategies a unit can adopt and this choice will, to a large extent, be influenced by the position on the matrix.

Build

You would mostly adopt a build strategy for a star or a question mark as gaining market share is much less costly when a market is growing rapidly, than when it is static or declining. Building tends to absorb cash in the short term, but the aim is that a unit which absorbs cash now will turn into a cash generator in the future. If a key competitor had become complacent or the development of a new technology had upset the equilibrium of a market, then you might find it profitable to use a build strategy in a low growth or shrinking market.

Harvest

Here you allow your market position to be eroded in order to transfer any cash generated to areas where it can be more profitably invested. You would normally harvest or 'milk' a cash cow.

Hold

If you are in a relatively strong position in a static market, you probably have a cash cow generating excess cash. While you may want to use much of this cash to grow stars and question marks, you will still reinvest just enough to protect your cash cow from competitive action and so maintain its market position.

Withdraw

Withdrawal may be necessary when you are in a weak position in a static market. Becoming profitable may require high investment and the unit might be consuming excessive management time compared to its low future potential. However, when withdrawing from an area a company should take care in prejudging a dog as being worth little, for the dog may be attractive to other companies who can gain synergies by acquiring it.

Summary

The above is, in some ways, a simplification of the BCG matrix. There have been several developments of the matrix. For example, the market growth and market share axes can be given scales, so that the precise position of a business in its quadrant exactly reflects its present market share and the percentage market growth. Also each business can be represented by a circle, whose area can indicate the sales volume. Thus businesses can be clearly compared with each other. Moreover the total portfolio of a company can be accurately displayed on one matrix helping identify any weakness or imbalances, for example too many cash cows or too many stars.

In addition, the four generic strategies – build, harvest, hold and withdraw – can have many different variations. A firm can, for example, build aggressively or gradually depending on its situation. It may build some parts of a product range, while simultaneously rationalizing others. It may build by injecting money, management, new ideas, existing or new products, expanding overseas, increasing production or marketing, cutting price, improving quality, licensing, forward or backward integration etc.

Implications

If you accept the portfolio analysis approach as being useful, it has a number of implications.

- An organization needs to have a balance in its portfolio between cash-generating and cash-absorbing units. Too many cash-using units may lead to bankruptcy, while too many cash-generating units may mean there is insufficient investment in the future.

- Any individual unit's strategy needs to be analysed to establish what effect it will have on the organization's overall portfolio.
- Acquisitions and divestments can be targeted to help provide a balanced portfolio of cash generators and users.
- Quite different goals can be given to different units as part of a total corporate plan – for example some (cash cows) may be permitted to lose market share, as long as they give a certain profit level, while others (stars) may be allowed to make a loss as long as they achieve a certain level of sales growth.

Strengths

- Portfolio analysis provided a simple, graphical way for larger organizations to visualize, understand and communicate the key characteristics of their product lines or units.
- It helped raise managers' strategic consciousness.
- It can be done on competitors to give an idea of their likely strategies.
- It is a useful tool for setting appropriate, distinct strategies for different units and deciding the needs of each.

In general, its major contribution was probably that it made managers aware of the dangers of investing too heavily in the 'safe' option of cash cows and starving the more risky stars and question marks, which would be the organization's future. It thus encouraged managers to think ahead, rather than automatically reinvesting resources in tried and tested areas which had been successful in the past. There are, however, a number of dangers in using portfolio analysis, and these are examined in the next chapter.

23
Portfolio analysis – alternative views

General Electric matrix

This matrix was originally jointly developed by the American General Electric Company and McKinsey and Co. consultants as part of the programme of splitting General Electric into strategic business units. The matrix helped assess how to divide corporate investment amongst the various business units.

Basically it is similar to the Boston Consulting Group matrix in that it has two axes against which products or business units can be plotted. The main difference is that instead of having just two variables – market growth and market share – as the two axes of the matrix, the General Electric matrix uses what have been called 'multiple factors'. There are two multiple factors – industry attractiveness and competitive position – and each of these is made up of a number of characteristics. For example, industry attractiveness includes the size and profitability of the industry, its growth rate, the nature and aggressiveness of the competition, the business cycle and the ability to gain economies of scale. Competitive position is made up of market share, profit level, management ability, production capability and technological strength.

Depending on the critical success factors in its industry, each company calculates its own way of measuring industry attractiveness and competitive position by giving weightings to each of the items which make up the two multiple factors.

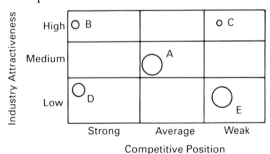

Figure 8 The basic General Electric matrix

Businesses or products can be represented by points or by circles, whose size indicates their relative sales turnover.

Those businesses in the upper left-hand section of the grid are those which should have the greatest potential and where investment should be channelled.

Those in the lower right are possibly candidates for divestment or at least harvesting. Although business B in the diagram is small in terms of turnover, it has a strong position in a highly attractive market. Business D, on the other hand, has a strong position, but probably in a declining or unprofitable industry. Business E has the second largest turnover, but is in a weak position in an unattractive industry. Investment should therefore mainly go to businesses B and C. The organization pictured possibly suffers from having most of its turnover in industries which are not very attractive.

Geographic analysis

The matrix format can be adapted to several different business situations. One common use is in helping decide investment or expansion into different geographical areas. Here market position can provide one axis and country attractiveness the other.

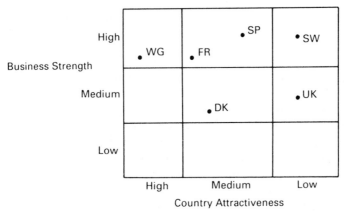

Key

FR – France
WG – West Germany
UK – United Kingdom
SW – Sweden
DK – Denmark
SP – Spain

Figure 9 Example of using a two-axis matrix to analyse geographical spread

Country attractiveness is usually a combination of economic growth, political stability, how favourable the environment is to business and overall market size. Business strength could include market share, profitability, distribution net-work, company image and suitability of the product to the population's life-style. As with the other grids, either a single point can be used to represent the position in each country of a product or business or else, to add accuracy, you can draw different-sized circles representing the relative turnover in each country. A further level of detail can be to have a circle for each country whose size represents the total market size, with a shaded segment showing what percentage of the total potential market your business or product accounts for.

Life-cycle analysis

This is a development of portfolio analysis normally associated with the business consultants Arthur D. Little. On this matrix the two axes against which a business or product is plotted are 'stage of the industry (product) life cycle' and 'competitive position'.

Competitive Position	Stage in the Life Cycle			
	Embryonic	Growth	Maturity	Ageing
Dominant				
Strong				
Favourable				
Tenable				
Weak				

Figure 10 Example of a life-cycle portfolio matrix

There are around twenty-five generic strategies which have been developed as part of this model. Once you have positioned your firm or product on the matrix, you then have a choice of four or five types of strategy which might be appropriate. For example, if you had a dominant position in an ageing market, you might want to defend your position, try and start a new life cycle by making a product or technological change, or focus on your most profitable items, allowing others to decline. But if you had a weak position in this market you would be foolish to invest and should probably try and rationalize to cut costs, possibly look to license or sell abroad, or even withdraw.

Weaknesses

Although portfolio analysis was at first seen as an important breakthrough in strategic thinking, it later attracted a great deal of criticism. Some of the main weaknesses are:

- There is a tendency for the process of portfolio analysis to become mechanistic. It can constrain managers' thought processes by appearing to give quick and easy analysis and solutions. So they end up with a limited set of options rather than being stimulated to think creatively.
- It only compares units against two main variables. By excluding many others, it may give a quite misleading image of reality and lead to inappropriate strategies – for example, you may be on the edge of a technological breakthrough in a business the matrix classifies as a dog. Or you may have strong innovative management in what technically is a cash cow. In both cases, portfolio analysis might lead you to overlook your key strengths.
- It can be misused by managers in search of an easy answer to complex issues. By concentrating on two axes it can allow a manager to take a simple view of what may in fact be a very intractable issue.

- It tends to cause several companies to adopt similar strategies. For example, in many industries, firms react to growth by heavy investment in increasing capacity. This quickly leads to overcapacity, price cutting to fill the capacity, reduced margins and disappointing returns. The supposed stars then turn out to be dogs. This is currently happening in the car industry and also in financial services.
- It becomes a self-fulfilling prophecy. If you have a cash cow and milk it, it will be prevented from growing. Likewise if you starve a business you believe to be a dog of cash, naturally it will decline. Whereas, if you had invested in them, they might well have given better returns than a star, which is usually a riskier investment.
- It may create motivational problems. Managers assigned to businesses which are viewed as cash cows or dogs will see that investment is always given to stars. They may then give up trying to build their businesses, become defeatist and thus accelerate decline rather than looking for ways to reverse it.
- It takes the past and projects it into the future without taking account of likely changes. It therefore tends to award investment according to past market growth and past performance rather than future potential.

An alternative view

It is possible to reverse the definitions of the four quadrants on the Boston Consulting Group matrix completely and thus come up with quite different strategies. For example:

Cash cows

Could be described as businesses where you have a strong position in a static market. You already have a great deal of experience in the industry – you have production facilities, a distribution network, knowledge of your customers, customer loyalty – in fact a firm basis on which to build. Therefore you should not milk this, but instead invest to develop new products and variants on existing products, which will benefit from all your accumulated experience and your facilities. Here there is no need to go through the costly process of building up production plants, a customer base or a distribution network – they already exist. No organization can expect to keep on picking winners with its stars, so you should instead turn your attention to new and creative ways of revitalizing cash cows and not squander resources on the risky stars.

Stars

These are in fast-growing markets. Fast-growing markets usually quickly attract a rush of competitors, all eager for what they see as an opportunity which is too good to be missed. They flood into the market (as happened with personal computers and electronic watches) creating overcapacity, low market share for everybody, low profits and often significant losses. Stars may turn out to be winners, but they can also be disasters which can distract too much management time and energy from the main task of running a profitable business.

Question marks

To be in a weak position in a growing market which is about to be flooded can hardly be seen as worthwhile. Sell your question marks to one of the new entrants, while they are still dazzled by the rapid market growth – you should get a good price as they are buying quick access to a market they think it is good to be in. It will be a while before they realize that, when the market is saturated, their hoped-for star has become a very hungry dog which will eat up all the resources they throw at it.

Dogs

You are in a weak position in a static market. Probably your competitors have become complacent. Or else they have put their best management into their stars, and their low performers into the static market. Also they have probably underinvested for years in their production facilities, their marketing efforts and their customer relationships. Although you are weak, they are probably both unprepared for and unable to deal with an attack. Therefore you should feed your dogs, invest in them, surprise the competition and probably get higher returns at a lower level of risk than with a star. Markets like zips, pianos and ball-bearings were typical dog markets until the Japanese saw their potential, attacked and quickly achieved a dominant position at the expense of sleeping American and European competitors.

This last section is designed to show that there should not be any automatic step between defining your business on a matrix and deciding an appropriate strategy. The crowd will always follow the obvious, easy route – the innovator will have to think more deeply before making his choice of strategy.

24
Industry structure analysis

This approach to the development of strategy was first proposed by Michael E. Porter from the Harvard Business School.[10] He argued that the reason different industries had quite different levels of profitability was due to differences in their basic economic structures. He proposed a method for analysing and understanding the forces which determined industry structure and thus profitability, to assist organizations in developing appropriate strategies.

An important innovation was the definition of competition. Porter proposed that competition was not just those firms making a similar product or offering a similar service, but all those organizations or groups which have the ability to affect the profits a firm could potentially earn in its industry. Thus customers or suppliers could both be seen as competitors as they are in competition with a firm for its profits – by charging a higher price a supplier can reduce a firm's profits, and likewise by pressing for price reductions a customer can have the same effect.

Porter identified five main forces which determine an industry's or firm's profitability – rivalry, buyer power, supplier power, new entrants and substitutes. To develop an effective strategy a firm had to analyse how each of these five forces could affect its profitability and then take action to defend itself or exploit the forces in its favour.

A brief description of how the five forces can affect profitability may be useful.

Rivalry

If one or two large companies dominate an industry, rivalry may be low and profitability high. However, if there are several nearly equal competitors there may be a continuous struggle to gain the upper hand by means of price wars, advertising battles and constant product refinement. In this case profits will tend to be depressed by the higher level of rivalry.

There are a number of factors which can increase the level of competition and thus reduce profits:

- If there is low or no growth in the industry, then the only means of expansion will be to steal market share from competitors.
- If competitors have had to make large investments in, for example, manufacturing plant, they may be anxious to recoup these by filling their capacity, often by using price-cutting.

- There may be internal 'political' or external political reasons why companies wish to be seen to have a strong presence in certain markets – the European Airbus is an example of the latter.
- If all the products on offer are fairly similar, price reductions may be one of the few ways of competing.

Buyer power

Buyers can have a high level of power to affect a firm's profitability if some of the following conditions are met:

- They are highly concentrated and buy large volumes.
- A firm has made a large investment in production facilities and is dependent on its buyers to fill capacity.
- Buyers can change suppliers without high switching costs. For example, changing from one computer supplier to another may involve a firm in expensive replacement of equipment and retraining of staff, while changing from one vegetable supplier to another may not involve much expense for a supermarket chain.
- Buyers can threaten backward integration, that is, doing the activity themselves – a car manufacturer, for example, may decide to make certain parts instead of buying them if it feels a supplier's price is too high.
- If the firm's product represents a high proportion of the buyer's cost, the buyer will tend to be more sensitive to the price.
- There are several firms supplying similar products.

However, if a firm's product is a relatively minor part of a buyer's costs or it is highly differentiated from competing products the firm may be able to avoid its profitability being severely affected by buyer power.

Supplier power

It is probable that suppliers' power will be high and that they can funnel off some of a firm's profits if:

- Suppliers are highly concentrated and/or do not compete aggressively with each other.
- They face no substitute products or alternative sources of supply – for example some suppliers have considerable control over sources of raw materials. Gold and diamond suppliers are typical cases.
- Switching costs from one supplier to another are high.
- Their products are highly differentiated, so it is difficult to obtain a similar product elsewhere.
- The firm or industry is not an important customer.
- The suppliers can threaten forward integration if they feel the prices they are receiving are not high enough or that there are good profits to be made.

New entrants

Even if it does not face strong buyers or suppliers and it is relatively concentrated and so partly free from destructive internal competition, an industry may not be able to make large profits, if these serve to attract new entrants. The threat of new entrants will vary according to the height of entry barriers. There are a number of potential barriers to entry including:

- There may be high capital requirements to start operating in a market, for example building a factory or having to launch a major advertising campaign.
- Economies of scale in production, distribution or marketing may give firms already in the industry cost advantages which a new entrant would have difficulty competing with.
- Firms in the industry may be blocking access to distribution channels. For example the major soap powder, toothpaste and soft drinks manufacturers each offer several competing brands, filling up supermarket shelf space and preventing new competitors gaining access to customers.
- Government policy, for example in the European airline industry, may restrict entry, allowing incumbents to charge higher prices than they could if in a competitive market.
- Existing products have high levels of differentiation and customer loyalty.
- There is a history of firms in the industry reacting aggressively to new entrants – in the grocery market for example, it is common for existing firms to start 'two for the price of one' offers to coincide with the launch of new competitive products, thus attracting customers away from the new offerings.
- Experience in the industry may give existing competitors an advantage over new entrants.

However, a shift in consumer tastes (from large cars to fuel-efficient cars in the 1970s) or in technology (from mechanical to electronic watches) can quickly cancel out the power of entry barriers. It may even give new entrants an advantage over existing competitors – for example a new production technology could make huge capital investments, by firms already in an industry, obsolete.

Substitutes

Firms in an industry may never be able to raise their prices and gain above average profits if there are existing or potential substitutes to their products. This is a situation faced by many food manufacturers and suppliers of entertainment like cinemas. A rise in price would cause some buyers to switch to alternative products.

Developing a strategy

Once a company has analysed the ways in which these five key forces can affect its ability to achieve high profits, it can start to develop a strategy. There are three main types of strategy a company can adopt to deal with these forces – pragmatic, manipulative or evolutionary.

Pragmatic strategy

Here the firm accepts the forces as they are and tries to find ways of working around them. It may decide to avoid taking its main competitors head-on, or else it might look for ways of reaching mutually beneficial arrangements with customers and suppliers, or it might even form alliances with existing competition or new entrants. In each case it is trying to reduce the power one of the five forces has to affect its ability to earn profits.

Manipulative strategy

The company may try to influence one of the forces. For example it might buy a supplier to secure materials, a customer to ensure access to its markets or companies which can supply substitutes to gain influence over their supply or pricing – advertising agencies have bought creative and media-buying agencies, paper manufacturers have purchased forests and oil companies have expanded into other sources of energy. A company may take over a competitor and thus reduce the level of rivalry or else gain cost, distribution or other advantages – Volkswagen bought the Spanish SEAT car company, Fiat bought Alfa Romeo and Ford took over Jaguar.

Evolutionary strategy

A company may identify that there are changes in the five forces and exploit these to gain advantage over competitors. For example, consumer interest in protection of the environment created a strategic window allowing new products access to supermarket shelves. Government legislation, regulation or deregulation can either strengthen existing competitors' positions or else remove barriers to entry allowing new entrants into previously restricted profitable industries.

Industry structure analysis can be a very powerful tool for analysing a situation and helping to develop strategy. Possibly it is more valuable than portfolio analysis, in that it goes deeper by examining the reasons why an industry or company earns a certain level of profits and thus provides leads as to what kind of strategy can protect a company from the main competitive forces which could erode its profitability.

25
Supply chain analysis

This is a method of analysing an organization's activities in order to develop actions and strategies to improve its competitiveness. Its basis is a view of the organization as a business system or series of activities, which is aimed at supplying 'value' to a customer. This value can be entertainment, saving time, utility, pleasure – in fact anything which is a reason why a firm or individual buys a product or service. A firm will be competitive in so far as it provides value as well as or better than other firms and is seen to do so by the consumer. Its profits will be determined by the extent the price the consumer is willing to pay, for the value he receives, exceeds the cost of supplying that value. Thus the two key elements an organization must devote its attention to are providing something which the consumer (rather than the organization) perceives to be value, and controlling the cost of providing that value. Nine out of ten new grocery products fail because, though the firm thinks it is providing value, the consumer sees no advantage in preferring the new product over existing offerings.

Supply chain analysis basically consists of examining all the activities which are involved in supplying a product or service to a customer, and determining how each activity adds value to the final product and whether this value sufficiently exceeds the cost of providing it. Some of these activities may take place inside the firm (production, marketing, distribution) and some may be outside the firm's direct control – for example obtaining raw materials and retailing goods may be beyond a manufacturer's scope of operations. But even if they are theoretically outside a firm's direct control, they can often still be influenced by the firm – a company can choose its suppliers and its methods of reaching its final customers.

Primary and support activities

In supply chain analysis an organization can be split into two parts. There are activities like goods receiving, manufacturing, distribution, marketing and after sales service which are directly concerned with producing and delivering the product. These are known as 'primary activities'. Then there are activities which support the primary activities such as human resource management, finance, technology development, procurement of resources and management systems.

The three main questions which need to be asked of each of these activities are

1. What value does it add for the final purchaser?

2. How does it help other activities provide value?
3. At what cost does it provide that value?

There are significant competitive advantages to be gained by rethinking the ways these activities can add value to the final product. For example, by establishing cooperative relationships with suppliers, rather than buying at the best price, many Japanese companies have managed to dramatically reduce inventory costs with 'just-in-time' component supplies. Virgin Airlines succeeded in overcoming the heavy capital investment costs involved in entering the airline industry by leasing, rather than buying, its planes. And the Swiss watch industry made a surprising recovery by rethinking the reasons why people bought watches – watches had developed from being expensive products bought for reliability to become lower price, fashion items.

Identifying value

Possibly one of the first steps in supply chain analysis is to identify what constitutes value for the consumer. Very often firms misjudge consumer perception of value because they fail to notice shifts in consumer priorities. For example, manufacturers of diesel cars are still talking of economy, when consumers are more interested in reducing pollution by buying lead-free petrol. Many manufacturers of industrial products fight desperately to reduce their costs and prices, while their customers are probably more interested in reliable deliveries, frequent deliveries, improved quality or faster response to product changes. And food manufacturers beaver away dreaming up ever more complicated prepared foods, while public taste is turning back towards fresh foods.

It is essential that a firm fully understands in what way its product or service brings value to the customer, if it is to improve competitiveness by increasing this value. For years makers of electric shavers have advertised how stylish their products were and what a close shave they gave, when their potential market (wet shavers) may have wanted a product that was convenient and did not irritate the skin. It is surprisingly common for firms to make inaccurate assumptions about why customers buy their products. One reason for this may be that those who built up the firm, and rose to positions of power with a particular business philosophy, find it difficult to adapt to new ways of serving the market. They therefore use their power to hold the firm to tried and tested methods.

Buyers will always operate with limited knowledge. They can never know the true value of a product, even after they have purchased it, as they can never totally compare it with alternative products. Therefore part of the buying decision and judgement of value will be based on perception. Another complicating factor is that in many purchases the buyer and user may be different. To create value, the organization must be aware of how buyers will ascribe value to their product – this is often not as straightforward as might at first be thought.

Primary activities

There are many ways in which the primary activities can create value for the customer. The most obvious would be to lower buyer cost. To do this all primary activities should be analysed to ensure they are working at optimum levels. Seasonality of demand may mean there are slack periods or else general demand levels may not fill capacity. Costs can be reduced by reducing capacity or subcontracting out spare capacity. Products can be redesigned to reduce production costs or else costs can be spread over greater turnover by exporting or licensing production abroad.

Whenever a buyer purchases a product there is always a certain element of risk that the product will not live up to his expectations. A firm can add value by reducing this risk through better after-sales service, more knowledgeable sales people, improving packaging and product information, providing training to the users, or increasing advertising specially in markets where advertising spend has traditionally been low.

Another approach would be to lower buyer effort. Better order processing and delivery, improved distribution, superior product performance or features, better after sales support, analysis of how the product is used and improvement of design, greater availability, faster delivery – all these can reduce the effort the buyer has to make in obtaining and using the product.

Support activities

Quite often support activities are not directly linked to creating value for the customer and their managers are not clear about how they fit in with the process of providing value. In fact, it can happen that the systems used actually restrict an organization's ability to provide value – for example, corporate pay and personnel policies can prevent a company being able to pay the market rate for good designers or engineers, or financial controls can stop key investments and slow down important research and development programmes.

If a firm analyses how its supply chain operates and what value it provides to customers, it then has a clear base against which managers of support activities can justify how they actively assist the process. Any activities they carry out, which either do not contribute to adding value to the supply chain or else obstruct the supply chain's functioning should be examined and if necessary changed or done away with. The only justification for support activities is that they do actually support the supply chain. If they do not then they just add unnecessary cost and complexity.

Linkages

A major area for increasing the value provided to customers is by improving the linkages between the different activities in the supply chain. These links can be divided into three main groups – links between an organization's suppliers and the organization, links between the activities occurring within the organization and downstream links between the organization, its distributors and its customers.

Links with suppliers

A great deal of work has been done in recent years by companies who have tried to move from having a competitive relationship to developing cooperation with suppliers. Instead of buying where the price was best, maintaining dual sources of supply and shifting suppliers when better offers were received, firms are trying to work with fewer suppliers on a more long-term basis. Also they are involving suppliers more in new product developments, treating them as partners and not adversaries. Some firms are starting just-in-time deliveries; others have linked up their production planning with suppliers and thus started automatic ordering instead of having to go through the administrative process of issuing purchase orders. And some suppliers deliver direct into firms' warehouses to always keep stocks at a certain agreed level, again avoiding administration time and costs.

Links within the organization

Often extra work or different ways of working in one department will save time and cost in another. Improved inspection at earlier stages of a process will be repaid by benefits later on, extra training for operators will result in higher output or better quality products, and improved communication will reduce the need for inventory and rework. Frequently standard accounting principles will work against improving linkages. By treating each department as a separate unit, requiring investments be recouped in a certain time-frame and only measuring tangible short-term, financial benefits, they can prevent actions which could significantly increase the perceived value to the customer. For example, greater investment in product design could save production costs in the medium or long term, but financial controls may stop the design department making the investment in changes.

Downstream links

Some firms take it for granted that once their product is sold it is the customer's problem. They thus fail to see all the opportunities there are for improving the value the customer receives. With industrial products, engineers could be sent to customers to train their staff or find technical improvements to help customers get the best from their purchases. Customers could be invited to your plant to see your processes and discuss any problems or ideas with your engineers and supervisors. You could even have a full-time engineer at a customer's plant to deal with any operating issues. You can set up joint projects with key customers for your mutual benefit or there are other ways you can think about the types of problem customers may be having and how you can help solve them – quality, faster delivery or whatever. You can also improve relations with consumers by offering wider service coverage and parts distribution, a twenty-four hour emergency service call facility, having comprehensible instructions with illustrations which someone who is not a technical genius may be able to understand, or having strong advertising to reassure customers who have bought your products that they made the correct decision.

Many services can also increase the value they deliver to their customers. Restaurants could give more information about the types of food they serve or more assistance with choosing wines. Medical services could become more actively involved in educating their clients in how to remain healthy. Financial institutions could provide more objective guidance on investment and on how customers can better control their personal finances. Shops could train their staff to give expert advice, help package or gift-wrap goods and improve their layout and sign-posting to save their customers' time.

Increasing the value your supply chain delivers to your customers can often be achieved at very little cost, but it can be quite effective in differentiating you from competitors and thus in building customer loyalty.

26
A definition of strategy

One business commentator noted that in the West the business of strategy development is growing rapidly, creating work for planners, consultants and academics. However the growth in the strategy market is not being matched by growth in the organizations who are buying strategy advice. In fact, Western companies are continuing to lose ground to Japanese, Korean and other competitors. Part of the reason for this situation may lie in how we understand and use the concept of strategy itself – because if we have a misguided view of what strategy is, the strategies we develop and the ways we implement them will also be wrong.

Top management usually makes the key strategic decisions

Western view of strategy

In the West we still tend to have hierarchical organizations with command and control structures. One recent book on strategy said that top management develops strategy, communicates it down to middle management to implement, and then controls the meeting of the plans. The assumption is that those at the top of the organization know best – yet they are not the people in daily contact with customers and suppliers, they are not the ones continuously experimenting with new product designs, and they are not those on the ground who constantly are forced to be aware of what competitors are up to.

A culture in which top management provides the answers and the rest of us obey and carry out our masters' bidding cannot function in a world of ambiguity, where there can be many answers and where the answer may constantly be changing. Hierarchical organizations need single, clear answers to questions of strategy. Thus every time a new technique is developed – corporate planning, decentralization into strategic business units, portfolio analysis, supply chain analysis, the pursuit of excellence, just-in-time, quality circles – managers rush at it, thinking they have finally found 'the solution' to their problems.

We are always looking for the 'one right answer' which will be developed by those above and then transmitted down through the organization. Thus we tend to develop strategies which are inviolable (they cannot be questioned by those below), are inflexible (they cannot rapidly adjust to changes in the market) and are not 'owned' by those who must implement them, as they had no part in their making. Coming, as they do, from above with, as it were, the Almighty's stamp of approval on them, our strategies – harvest, build, diversify, withdraw or whatever – tend to act as constraints within which people must work rather than as stimuli to encourage contribution. They also often only reflect the interests of top management and shareholders – improve profitability by 10 per cent, improve yield on shares by 20 per cent – when they should be giving the lower ranks a goal to motivate them.

What strategy should not be

Rather than falling into the 'one right answer' trap of trying to define what strategy is, it may be more useful to give some examples of what it should not be:

- It should not be primarily focused on keeping up with the competition and matching their every move – starting just-in-time because they do, cutting costs when they cut, using quality circles because they are. Imitative strategies leave you trailing behind competitors, because you are chasing a moving target. By the time you catch up with what they are doing today, they will be on to something new.
- It should not be so carefully planned and tested against all eventualities that it avoids innovation, excitement and risk.
- It should not be purely based on 'strategic fit' – analysing what the organization is capable of and then designing a strategy to match. This approach assumes the organization cannot improve, but will always stay as it is.
- It should not be only aimed at increasing shareholder wealth or satisfying top management ego.
- It should not be mainly focused on short-term profits to satisfy the financial markets and bolster share price.

- It should not be built on the assumption that top management are omniscient or that they will get it right every time.
- It should not be developed mechanistically by using one or other of the many invitingly clever models which are available
- It should not assume that dominating a market or beating competitors is always the best policy. Many markets can be profitable when in a state of near equilibrium, but as soon as one firm starts a price, new product or advertising battle the profits are squandered on pointless antagonism.
- It should not be some great future vision which nobody seriously believes in.
- It should not change wildly with every shift in top management or remain rooted in some great glorious past which has long since been history.

Going back to basics

We have become so inebriated by the brilliance of all the different strategic models we have created, that we have lost sight of some basic realities of business life:

Serving the customer

A firm generates its income from serving its customers, not from trying to annihilate the competition. You don't serve your customer better by indulging in massive advertising fights to the death, nor by cajoling or bribing him into buying your product. You do it by finding out what he wants from your type of product and then looking for ways to provide this better than the competition. A vast amount of market research goes into testing how consumers respond to various advertising campaigns; too little is directed at deep analysis of how products can be improved. There is a need for companies to rethink what their products do and thus how they can better serve their customers. If you serve your customer better than your competitors do, then beating the competition becomes a side-effect of greater customer satisfaction, not your aim in life.

Need for innovation

Any concept a company develops which gives them a competitive advantage will quickly be copied by competitors. In fact competitors may even have an advantage, as they can imitate a ready-made product they know consumers want and so avoid heavy research and development costs. Thus there is no point throwing most of an organization's resources at developing the ultimate product which will deliver a body-blow to your competitors – you will just be disappointed when the great coup fails to materialize. Instead you should expect that to remain competitive, you must be able to innovate continually, which means being able to be creative, to admit mistakes and to learn new skills. It is not obvious that 'top-down' strategies can permit this kind of constant flexibility and improvement.

Elements of strategy

This leads to starting to define some of the characteristics an organization's strategy should contain.

Customer orientation

It should be aimed first and foremost at identifying and satisfying customer needs. For example, harvesting has been proposed as a strategy – yet harvesting means that a firm believes there is no possible way it can better satisfy customer needs, so it wants to get out as much as it can while it can. Harvesting is not a strategy, it is an attitude of defeatism, which denies the possibility of creativity, innovation and changes in customer needs in a mature industry sector. Only by identifying and satisfying customer needs will you be profitable, beat the competition and ensure your own survival – harvesting cannot be the way to achieve this.

Continuous learning

A strategy must be aimed at developing the organization's ability to continuously monitor its customers and environment, to learn from what it finds out and to adapt to changing circumstances. A strategy must therefore be able to take all the signals coming in throughout the organization and channel them into positive action. It must treat information coming into the organization as opportunities to be seized, rather than unpleasant and threatening facts to be denied.

Synergies

A group of people, company management for example, who all have similar backgrounds, similar experiences and similar points of view may easily come to agreement on strategy. But they are unlikely to develop good strategies. A rounded strategy is the result of many different viewpoints from several levels of the organization. It is the result of constructive conflict, not passive agreement. Good strategy is created by synergies between the members of an organization, not similarities.

Unification and motivation

A strategy should offer something to all the company, a goal they can all relate to and not just be a series of financial targets, which have to be met. It should also provide a clear direction, so all departments can identify whether they are working with or against the overall company strategy. If their systems and behaviours are impeding the implementation of the strategy, then they need to be adjusted. Moreover the organization's system of recognition and rewards should actively support the behaviours which are in line with its strategy – too often these work against each other.

Organizational stretch

A strategy should not just 'fit' current organizational abilities, assuming no possibility of improvement. Instead it should challenge or stretch the organization so that people, systems and products have to develop and improve, instead of being expected to remain static.

Winning

A strategy should try and create some kind of team spirit in an organization and provide a series of goals so that people can feel their efforts are leading to some result. People need to feel they are part of a winning team and not just functionaries carrying out the wishes of others.

Participation

Strategy must be built upon participation. Top management may want to set general guidelines, but people below must feel they have some freedom within these guidelines and also the power to influence strategic direction. In particular, when people 'on the floor' pick up signals which suggest that the strategy may not be correctly focused or that there may be new opportunities which were not previously identified, there must be mechanisms to encourage them to feed this back, so that any necessary adjustments can be made. Many events which will affect a company may happen outside management's field of vision. When these events are sensed by anyone, there must be some way this information can be passed back up the organization.

Management stability

Good strategy cannot be developed and implemented by managers following an upward career path, which means they spend only two to three years in any job, before expecting promotion. Such managers will tend to look for quick short-term, bottom-line results to fuel their next career move – so they will cut costs and research and development, rather than looking for ways to build the organization's future.

Development of employees

A strategy should have the intention of training and developing employees, of teaching them new skills, of investing in the organization's human capital. It should not just be based on obedience and control.

Summary

Of the four basic strategies proposed by one strategy model, three – harvest, hold, withdraw – are basically defeatist. They are signs that an organization has given up the battle. Thus it is little wonder that Western organizations using such models are losing out to their competitors.

In fact there can only be one defensible strategy. That is to build an organization that is capable of learning, adapting and improving, an organization that is not constrained by top management's control, but which is open and flexible enough to admit mistakes and rethink its position. Such an organization will automatically find the right actions to take, because it is built up of so many different people all sensing changes and opportunities in the environment. This may sound idealistic, but some organizations – especially Japanese companies like Honda and Yamaha – have achieved this. Honda moved from motorbikes to cars, and Yamaha from motorbikes to pianos, displaying a flexibility and adaptability few Western competitors could match. An organization where a great voice from on high suddenly decrees 'decentralize' or 'centralize' or 'diversify' or 'rationalize' or whatever will usually be insensitive to its environment and continuously be caught out by the flexibility of its competitors.

27
Managing turnaround

Many people will live through organizational decline during their working lives. In some cases this decline will be reacted to and reversed; in others it will be ignored for too long and may lead to the demise of a division or a whole organization. Organizational decline is not as inevitable as some managers of afflicted organizations would like to believe. It usually starts when changes in the environment highlight the inflexibility of an organization which cannot change. Although managers of suffering organizations may believe they are the victims of circumstances and can only adopt a defensive stance and try to slow down the decline, many of their competitors will be prospering at their expense. This suggests that the cause of decline will most often lie within top management and not further down the organization or outside it.

Reasons for decline

The main reasons for decline include:

- a failure to adjust resources to levels of demand, for example firms who do not react to changes in the economic cycle;
- having inadequate sensors of changes in the environment or else no mechanisms for transmitting knowledge of changes back up through the organization;
- slowness in response to changes in the environment, in spite of awareness of them;
- high level of gearing when faced with an economic downturn;
- the strategy-making body is too limited – for example, it may consist of one person (a strong chairman) or a small group of directors, who all think in similar ways;
- overtrading: activity increases faster than the resources to fund that activity, so there is a liquidity crisis;
- lack of learning, when competitors are improving quality, technology or efficiency;
- management adopt a defeatist strategy – harvesting, holding or withdrawing – and by cutting off investment, condemn an organization to (often unnecessary) decline.

Reactions to decline

An awareness of the various negative reactions to decline can help identify these and try and prevent them. Some of the most common are:

Top management

- have reached their positions by doing business in a certain way and so cannot understand any need to change;
- see decline as just a little temporary difficulty which can be dealt with by cutting costs ('tightening belts');
- believe the crisis is due to efforts to change the organization and so move to regain control and impose their traditional policies;
- start creative accounting – revaluing property, spreading R & D costs over a long period, giving financial institutions over-optimistic forecasts;
- defend the strategies for which they are responsible, as they think they will be blamed if the strategies are seen to be wrong.

Human resources

- throughout the organization people will be aware of the problems and of management's inability to react; frustration and defeatism will grow and the effort they make will decline;
- the best people will leave, giving you the problem of how to manage turnaround with lower calibre staff.

Politics

The feeling of limited resources and sense of frustration and pressure will exacerbate existing conflicts. Moreover, conflicts will become more personal rather than interdepartmental. There may also be a search for scapegoats. People's energy will be sucked into defending their positions rather than trying to cooperate with each other.

Structure

There is a shift of power from the wealth-creating areas to administrative areas, as increased control and cost-cutting start. Normally reductions in central administration are less than those made in operating areas, so the situation is worsened as a smaller group is left supporting an unproductive centre.

Cost-cutting

This begins gradually and management promises that each wave of rationalization will be the last. But because they lack courage and proceed slowly, there are a series of cost reductions. People lose trust in management, are afraid, give up hope and passively expect failure.

Managing growth and managing decline require different approaches

Dealing with decline

This is similar to other forms of organization change. The difference is that as it is done under severe time and financial constraints, people's participation and learning may have to be sacrificed to the necessity for rapid results.

Replace top management

It seems to be a prerequisite of successful turnaround that top management are replaced. They are responsible for the policies which have failed, they have ignored the need for change or else prevaricated, they represent the types of behaviour which have led to decline and they have tried all the solutions they can think of. If you only replace one or two members of the management group, the new arrivals may not have the critical mass to shift the others. Moreover the survivors will tend to defend their former policies, criticize the turnaround policies and create dissension and confusion. Also, it is a necessary signal to those below that change is a reality – if they still see some of the same faces at the top, they will not believe that policies and behaviour must be altered.

Another reason for a change in management is that the new management should have experience of turnaround situations. These require quite different skills and policies to managing growth or stability and the existing management is unlikely to understand or possess the necessary competencies.

Other management tasks

The new top management needs to show clear leadership. It is probably too late to pass the problem down to the organization by encouraging participation.

Moreover, people would most likely believe that they are being given management's problems, only without management's rewards.

The new management also should express a belief in the future and not just fuel decline by talking about cost reduction and control without providing a positive vision to balance the temporary pain.

The people who will manage the turnaround at various levels in the organization must be identified, be given roles which are different from their previous roles and have their new responsibilities clearly explained to them. If possible they should be given salary increases to indicate that their positions are safe and to discourage them from leaving. This may also work to show others that they are less valuable and they may decide to leave of their own accord.

If there are to be redundancies, there should only be one round of personnel reductions. It is better to cut too deeply and then have to rehire selectively, than to have the fear, demotivation and distrust which successive waves of cuts will cause. Any redundancy programme should affect unproductive central support functions at least as much as productive departments.

Short-, medium- and long-term actions

Short term (1–3 weeks)

The immediate issue in a turnaround may be to ensure the survival of the business. This would include:

- Take immediate financial control – reduce authority to spend, cut all entertainment, travel, recruitment and temporary staff, and focus resources on cash collection from debtors.
- Understand the sales situation. Do not listen to top and upper-middle management – they took the firm to where it is and will have many ingenious explanations of why and how complex things are and how many problems they have, etc. Summon the sales staff, hear the reality of bad quality, late deliveries, uncompetitive products or whatever – so you know what you are dealing with. In particular investigate the costing system and product margins – it is likely products are not being costed properly, that people do not actually know what the high margin items and loss-making items are and that the sales force are being rewarded on the basis of total turnover sold rather than profit margins generated. If this is the case change the sales-force bonus system. When the personnel director says this is impossible, change him.
- Ask each department for cost reduction recommendations and also for a full justification of their existing costs.

Medium-term (3–8 weeks)

- Implement a cost-reduction programme.
- Review each department's contribution to the business, looking particularly for ways that systems and attitudes prevent effectiveness. See how they

measure their own effectiveness and improve effectiveness measurements if necessary.

- *Marketing*. Investigate what effects a 10, 20 or 30 per cent decrease in the marketing budget would have. If this will be limited, then implement it. Also examine how marketing and advertising effectiveness is measured. For example, is most of your market research concentrated on your advertising and not your products, and are you just trying to match your competitors' spend rather than looking for creative ways to produce a better effect with less money? Establish who really controls your advertising spend, your advertising agency or you.
- *Production*. Look for ways to reduce overtime, increase output, improve quality without major capital expenditure. Try to reduce stock and identify and reduce the main bottlenecks. If minor expenditure can produce quick results authorize this.
- *Administration*. Question the necessity and frequency of all activities.
- All managers should submit improvement plans by the end of this period detailing how, now that cost reductions have taken place, they intend to start revitalizing their areas.

Longer-term (after 2 months)

- Rewrite the year's budget to reflect the new reality.
- Develop a clear strategy for the future which can be reactive to changes in the environment.
- Start to loosen control and encourage people throughout the organization to contribute and develop.
- Broadcast any successes to encourage further efforts and communicate the message that past mistakes have been realized.
- Start a series of new projects, with teams of people from several functions to give people something positive to focus their efforts and to try to start breaking down previous patterns of failure.

MARKETING

28 The marketing concept

29 Differential advantage

30 Developing a marketing strategy

31 Consumer behaviour

32 Setting prices

33 Marketing and the product life cycle

34 Industrial marketing

35 Marketing services

36 Writing a marketing plan

28
The marketing concept

Throughout the 1950s and early 1960s consumer demand for products tended to equal or outstrip industry's capacity to supply. So Western management focus concentrated on improving production facilities to increase output and meet this demand. However, during the late 1960s and the 1970s economic growth began to slow, supply of many items was in excess of demand, markets became saturated and new, international (mainly Japanese) competitors established a strong presence in Western markets. This led to an increase in competition and a shift in management attention away from the logistics of production to the problem of how to perform more effectively in the market-place.

There is a difference between marketing and selling

The marketing concept is that firms will be successful only in so far as they understand and respond to the needs of buyers better than their competitors. Although this may seem like common sense, many firms have not understood the full implications of this and still only pay lip service to it. Adopting the marketing concept means accepting a total business philosophy according to which all areas of an organization have the primary goal of satisfying customer needs. Some companies still see marketing as a mixture of sales, PR and advertising which is at the end of the product development and introduction process, rather than viewing it as the driving force of the whole business.

Product, production and selling orientations

Although most companies think they are marketing-oriented, it is common to find that in fact they are really driven by other priorities. The most usual are product, production and selling.

Product

A product-oriented firm is one that becomes too involved in developing the best product. It inherently believes that consumers will want the product with the best features, quality, performance or whatever. This kind of company is always surprised when a competitor is first to market and is more successful even though offering what the product-oriented firm believes to be an inferior product. Business history is full of instances where companies who first developed or improved products were not those who gained the market advantages of their work.

Production

The economies of scale which can be gained from mass production put intense pressure on some companies to produce large volumes of products at low cost. The belief is that if the product is cheap enough and widely available, it will readily find a market. Often there will be considerable conflict in firms between marketing's desire to offer a greater range or more features and the economics of production which favour standardization. Moreover mass production techniques push some companies away from true marketing and towards selling what they can produce most cheaply.

Selling

Some firms almost seem to operate in the belief that if you advertise and sell hard enough, you will manage to shift your product. Others just confuse marketing with selling. In a world where most markets are highly competitive, it is easy to begin to think that success goes to he who sells most effectively.

Marketing orientation

In fact, the marketing concept is the opposite of the selling orientation. The marketing concept is based on the idea that if you successfully identify and satisfy your customers, there will be no need to sell – good marketing should make selling unnecessary. In the marketing concept a transaction with a customer should be an exchange which leaves both parties feeling better off. In selling, one person tries to get another to purchase something he does not really want. Selling sees the customer as a target and a victim; marketing sees him as a source of ideas and an investment to be cultivated, because he will talk about his satisfaction with the product (or service), recommend it and buy other products from the same company. A person may buy six or seven cars in a lifetime – if one car firm can keep him as a loyal customer, he will represent a considerable source of income. Likewise a shopper in a supermarket should not be seen as a one-off transaction, but as a potential customer who may buy considerable quantities weekly for several years.

Existing and latent markets

There are two main types of market a company can choose to operate in – existing and latent. Existing markets are those where products and their benefits are well known by consumers, and would include most groceries and other household goods. Latent markets are consumer needs which are not yet satisfied until a new product or service is introduced – highlighters, Post-It notes, the Apple personal computer and the Sony Walkman all identified latent markets.

Most business takes place in existing markets. And most new products are launched into them, as firms prefer the safety of known territory. However, competing in an existing market can be extremely expensive, as you usually have to take market share from others by means of price and advertising battles. So the 'easy option' often fails to be as profitable as first forecast.

To compete in latent markets requires effort and innovation to discover and meet new consumer needs. However, the rewards can be enormous, as you will initially operate in a market with little or no competition and so you can set higher prices than you could if you were fighting many competitors. There are several ways of developing latent markets – it can be through new products, but may also be through finding new methods of distribution or new retailing formulas. True marketing is the discovery and exploitation of latent markets, but most firms spend their time imitating other firms in existing markets, rather than trying to innovate to develop latent markets.

Non-product marketing

This is a description of a strategy taken by many companies. Instead of seriously working to identify and satisfy customer needs, firms either make minor cosmetic changes to products and launch them as 'new!' or else embark on advertising and/or price wars in the hope of increasing market share without making any change to the product. Non-product strategies are so called because they are not based on offering any real product improvement. Such strategies are particularly encouraged by advertising and sales promotion agencies – they usually receive a percentage of their clients' spend and so are interested in this being as high as possible. It would be much less in their interest if clients were to invest more in new product development.

Most non-product strategies are ultimately unsuccessful. Either the customer sees that there is little or no added benefit in the 'new, improved' product, or else competitors respond by increasing their advertising spend or decreasing their prices. Then the battle becomes a 'zero sum competition' where firms compete away their profits without ending up any better off. The marketing concept highlights the importance of having a true, rather than imaginary, product to offer to the market. Clever advertising and gimmicky sales promotion tend to fool the companies throwing money at them, more than they fool consumers.

Left- and right-brained approaches to management

This theory suggests that there are two types of approach a firm can take when developing strategies for improving profitability. The left side of the brain is the one which controls our numerical and analytical functions and the right side that which is responsible for our creative, artistic and musical abilities. Left brain management is concerned with improving performance through financial control and rationalization. It can usually show a rapid result in terms of a firm's financial performance. However, such a strategy is often short-term in that it tends to result in stabilizing or reducing a firm's activities and thus does not build for the future. Many European and American companies adopted this approach, when their profitability was affected by Japanese competition.

Right-brained management is concerned with the identification and satisfaction of customer needs, innovating rather than controlling, growing rather than contracting. Right-brained strategies take longer to implement and show less clear results. Right-brained strategies would typically aim at expansion through gaining market share. In the short term they may be unprofitable as increasing market share can be expensive. But, as many Japanese firms have shown, once a company dominates a market it can be extremely profitable and difficult to dislodge from its position.

In the West, where many marketing managers only expect to remain in a job for two or three years, there is a tendency to adopt left-brained tactics to make a quick mark – cut down on new product development, reduce other operating costs and maybe throw money at campaigns to gain short-term increases in market share (non-product strategies). But such an approach is sacrificing the firm's future in the interests of producing rapid results. It is essential that more firms move away from the short-term left-brained policies, which lead to retrenchment and contraction, and start focusing more on right-brained longer-term growth strategies.

29
Differential advantage

Perfect competition and monopoly

There are two extremes between which any market can fall. Perfect competition occurs when there are many producers offering identical or very similar (commodity) products; monopoly is when only one firm offers a unique product. Under perfect competition, consumers will tend to prefer one product to another on the basis of price and no producer can make large profits. In monopoly consumers must either take the product at the price offered, or else do without or buy a substitute. Firms with monopolies or near monopolies (gas, electricity, water) can usually make large profits.

Most firms try to create a differential advantage (DA) for their products – this is a reason why (apart from price) consumers should prefer their products to those of competitors. By creating a DA, firms create a situation of imperfect competition or quasi-monopoly, where the customer believes he cannot obtain the same benefits from any other product or service; he will therefore be prepared to pay more for it and not switch to a competitor for minor price differences. Perfume companies are experts at creating a DA, for what many people believe to be essentially similar products, by building images around their products. Petrol companies spend large amounts claiming a DA for their brands, when in fact several brands often come from the same refinery. There may be minor differences in the additives each company uses, but it is not clear the public believes that any particular brand has a DA over the others, in spite of the petrol companies' massive advertising and promotional campaigns.

Sources of DA

Differential advantage can come from any aspect of a product or service – its wide availability (Coca-Cola), its convenience (Apple computers), its style (Ferrari cars), its quality (Rolex watches), good parts availability (Caterpillar), a large service network, the range of sizes or whatever. And the more levels of DA a product or service has, the greater will be the tendency of customers to prefer it to rivals and so the greater will be its degree of protection against price warfare.

Many firms confuse extra features or superior performance with DA. For example, car manufacturers often claim that their model can go from start to a certain speed in so many seconds. While this may well be true, it is not certain that most potential customers perceive this as a good reason for buying that particular model. To be a real DA, a feature has to be important to the customer and be perceived as important by the customer – it has to make the customer really believe he is getting some added value. Many new products fail because the different features they offer are not perceived by the customer to be worth switching from a known brand or paying a premium price.

Communicating DA

In an overcommunicated society, the noise level from competing products' advertising is so high that it can be very difficult to be heard. Yet a firm cannot assume its products' DA will be perceived by the customer – it has to be marketed and sold. Much marketing of DAs is weak because it concentrates on the features of the product rather than the benefits. A customer is not interested in performance characteristics in themselves – he is interested in their results, what they will do for him – save time, make him extra profits, allow him to produce better quality, help him look, smell or feel better. A common mistake is to concentrate on the features, without explaining why they are important.

Firms should be careful not to over-communicate DA by claiming too much for the product. This is an easy trap to fall into when competitors, who may have little or no DA to offer, are making inflated statements about their products. However, customers tend to see through advertising hyperbole – especially if they buy the product and are then disappointed. Also firms should not try and communicate too many DAs at one time. People pick up a very small part of the advertising they see and will tend to remember only products where there is one clear message.

As DA is very dependent on the perception of buyers you may have to manage this perception to get customers to value the DA you are offering. Volvo have done this successfully by selling the importance of safety. A customer who begins to value safety higher than style or performance will naturally gravitate towards buying a Volvo.

DA as a basis for strategy

The business and marketing strategy any firm adopts is essentially determined by its products' DAs. If some products have little or no DA, then they will tend to fall into a commodity market, where price will determine consumer choice and profits will be low. If a product has a strong, sustainable DA which the customer values, then proper communication and marketing of this should ensure above average profits. Only by creating true, sustainable DA can a firm obtain reasonable profitability. So a firm's strategy must be built around developing and defending DA for each product or else offering commodity products at a lower price than competitors. Moreover the type of DA you offer will to a great extent decide who your customers are, in which markets you can compete and at what price levels.

DA and repositioning

Any product's DA will gradually be eroded by such factors as competitors' copying, new technologies, new superior DAs, or strong price competition.

Also consumer tastes may change and a gap will develop between the needs of the market and what a firm is offering, as happened with European motorcycle manufacturers who believed customers wanted their famous brand names and craftsmanship, when taste had moved towards cheaper, higher performance Japanese models.

Therefore a firm needs to continually assess whether the DA it is offering is still of value to its customers and to try and build new DAs as barriers to competitive pressure. If the DA is losing some of its power, then the firm may have to redesign the product or else reposition it so that it offers a DA customers are more likely to value. Some firms have successfully repositioned well-known products every five to ten years to give them new leases of life – many traditional food manufacturers, caught out by the rise of prepared foods, have made a come-back by targeting their products at people looking for healthier foods, Marks and Spencer have continuously adjusted their range to match changing consumer trends which have hurt other retailers and drink manufacturers like Martini and Gordon's Gin are adept at changing the image of their offerings to fit in with changing consumer tastes.

30
Developing a marketing strategy

Few people will have the opportunity to develop a new marketing strategy for a totally new product. Most marketing work will be done on existing or improved products, which are already part of well developed strategies. However, it may still be useful to go through the seven major steps involved in developing a marketing strategy as many existing strategies can have significant weaknesses in one or more of the main stages. Comparing existing strategies to the model can help to highlight these weaknesses and guide what action should be taken.

1. Developing the strategic objective

This is the overall marketing goal of the firm – to expand market share, to increase the market, to take share from competitors, to develop a new level of differential advantage, to cut investment to maximize short-term profit, and so on. The strategic objective will depend on the degree of growth or decline in the market, the firm's competitive position, the level of competition and the sustainability of the firm's differential advantage. For example, one product may have a strong position in a growing market and another an average position in a static market. But if the level of competition is much higher in the growing market, it may be that the product in the static market will be more profitable until there is a shake-out in the growing market which causes some weaker competitors to withdraw. So the firm may have quite different strategies for the two products.

There is a tendency for Japanese companies to have growth in market share as a strategic objective and, encouraged by a financial system which takes a long-term view, they will often sacrifice short-term profits (sometimes for several years) in order to gain a dominant position in a market. Western companies, pressurized by financial markets which require quarterly, half-yearly and annual results to constantly show certain profit levels, will focus more on extracting short-term profits to protect their share value – if this is allowed to drop, they may become vulnerable to take-over.

2. Deciding the strategic focus

Strategic focus is how a firm will achieve its strategic objective – for example by selling the concept of the product to stimulate demand, by stronger branding and promotion to win competitors' customers or by improving productivity to increase profits in a price-sensitive market. The strategic focus will depend mainly on the stage of the product life cycle (see Chapter 33, Product Life Cycle) and the market segments in which a firm is operating. In the early stages of the product life cycle (introduction and the first part of growth) there are usually few competitors and so a firm will tend to try to extend usage by selling the concept to convert non-users and enter new market segments. As growth slows and the market becomes mature, the firm will tend to move to selling its brand rather than the generic product idea and will try to build brand loyalty and increase usage rate. In mature and declining markets, profitability can be increased in three main ways – gaining part of competitors' market share, holding market share and reducing costs, or developing a new version of the product to start a new product life cycle.

3. Choosing customer targets

The firm must clearly define who its customer targets are and what differential advantage the product will give each target market segment. The same product can often have different differential advantages in different market sectors – for example, an industrial robot may be sold to smaller firms through providing technical help and to a large company on the basis of delivering consistent quality on large volumes of similar items. Or a piece of hi-fi equipment may appeal to specialists because of its performance characteristics but to the general public due to looks or ease of use.

It is not sufficient to talk of general demographic categories like housewives or C1/C2 men or families with two children. Markets are increasingly splitting into different consumer groups with different aspirations, life-styles and expectations from products. Choosing customer targets means analysing how the market is segmented, what the needs of each segment are, what are the relative sizes and profitabilities of each segment, how purchasing decisions are made and how the firm's differential advantage(s) can be most successfully exploited in the market. Too many companies just offer a range of products to 'the market' without thinking through exactly what benefits they are providing to which market sectors.

4. Choosing competitor targets

A marketing strategy should also include a comprehensive review of who the main competitors are and what their strategies are. This has several aims – to help decide how to position a product to avoid head-on conflict with a strong competitor; to identify any strategic windows, gaps in the market not fully served by other product offerings; and to anticipate whether competitors are aggressive in increasing market share, imitators, price fighters or harvesting.

Competitors can be good or bad. Good competitors are those who are content to let the market remain in equilibrium, so that all competitors can make reasonable profits. Bad competitors are firms who constantly engage in price and advertising battles and who force other firms to compete away their profits.

Sometimes firms make the mistake of attacking good competitors and driving them towards bankruptcy, so they are bought by larger companies who then embark on aggressive market domination strategies.

When analysing competitors, companies need to look beyond the narrow view that competitors are firms offering similar products. Customers do not buy products; they buy ways of satisfying certain needs. Therefore anything that can satisfy the need which a firm's product is aimed at is also a competitor. Buses, trains and planes are competitors to cars – many Western countries are moving to reduce road congestion with higher petrol taxes and investment in public transport. Records do not just compete with other records, but also with other forms of entertainment and other ways people have of making statements about themselves.

5. Deciding on the product offering

The market strategy should be quite clear about how the product offered will both distinguish itself from competitive products and answer identified customer needs. This part should include a description of how this happens currently and how it is expected to develop over the next few years.

A typical Japanese strategy in the 1960s and 1970s was to develop a product which offered reasonable quality and performance at a low price, to target the lower end of the market, to gradually move up market from the lower price to higher price segments, forcing Western companies to retreat segment by segment, and then finally to arrive at a situation where they dominated the market and where their differential advantage had moved from reasonable quality at low price to high quality at average to above average price.

6. Developing the marketing mix

The marketing mix is a description of the four key areas of the marketing plan – deciding what exactly the product and its differential advantage are to be, fixing a price, setting a promotion budget and splitting this between above-the-line (advertising) and below-the-line (sales promotion and PR) and deciding on methods of distribution. These are commonly called the four Ps of marketing – product, price, promotion and place.

The firm must ensure that there is a fit between these four elements – a high price high quality product should be promoted in media which enhance its image and sold through outlets which reflect the image. Although this seems obvious, there are often cases where firms bring out a new product which is in a different price or image group from their existing range or which appeals to a slightly different market segment. But because they already have a sales organization and distribution network they use that, even if it is inappropriate. For example, one company had photocopier sales reps trying to sell its new range of computers while another had the same marketing department handling low price, high volume cars and also high price luxury cars. In both cases, the arrangement broke down because quite different attitudes, skills and contacts were required. When Honda and Nissan both launched their luxury car ranges in the USA, both set up separate dealer networks from their volume car ranges. They understood that the new models would go to a different type of customer and so would need a different approach and different selling styles.

7. Implementation and control

The final part of developing a marketing strategy is to determine how this will be implemented and controlled. There should be a clear identification of roles and responsibilities, strategic milestones, how achievement will be measured and what types of corrective action can be taken if expected results are not achieved. Too often marketing strategies do not include a sufficiently detailed analysis of how performance will be monitored. The result is that failure to meet objectives is not identified and it is not till the end of the financial year, that the size of the problem is realized.

Conducting an organization audit

If the whole organization is based on the principle of supplying value to the customer more effectively than the competition, then this can be used as a basis for a regular annual audit. Total organization performance should first be measured in terms of market share and profitability. Then the individual departments' contribution to this goal can be judged and opportunities for improvements identified and acted on.

Particular emphasis should be placed on defining how the market has changed during the year, what actions competitors have taken and what implications these have for the firm.

Importance of being brand leader

An issue which many companies overlook in their marketing strategies is the importance of being brand leader. A large number of firms are content to remain second, third or fourth in a market without realizing the disadvantages this puts them at. Studies have shown that the brand leader in many markets is two to three times as profitable as the second brand, even if the second brand's sales are near the level of the brand leader's.

The main advantage of being brand leader is that unit costs are lower – even if several brands have similar production costs, by having a high volume of sales over which to spread selling, distribution and advertising costs, the leader can gain cost advantages. This advantage is greatly increased by the nature of the distribution and display system. Limited retail space reduces the number of brands which can be displayed. The brand leader can normally obtain space in most outlets. But the second or third brand may have to negotiate hard to be given space and will often have to make significant price concessions. The fourth or fifth brand have virtually no negotiating power and will have trouble achieving profitable arrangements. This situation is worse when large retailers want to sell their own (more profitable) brands. In this case, it may only be the brand leader, and the retailer's own brand which are stocked.

Many firms' struggle to make acceptable profits can thus stem from the fact that they failed to establish their products as dominant brands during the growth stages of markets and so never manage to achieve a favourable cost structure or strong negotiating position to bargain with their stockists.

31
Consumer behaviour

Push versus pull marketing

There are two opposed styles of marketing. A 'push' marketing strategy is based on selling large volumes of usually fairly standardized goods, normally by means of heavy advertising and/or low pricing (discounts, special offers, etc.). 'Push' marketing is based on the belief that the firm can to a great extent influence potential customers' needs and behaviour. A 'pull' approach sees the customer as being more independent-minded. It aims at adjusting the firm's product offerings to meet identified customer needs, rather than trying to persuade the customer to buy what the firm can provide. Most firms would claim they have 'pull' marketing. However the huge amounts of money spent on 'hard sell' advertising for undifferentiated products, the large number of not very new 'new' products and the vast variety of special offers and gimmicky promotions suggest that many marketers still adopt a 'push' attitude.

Nevertheless, the increasing level of competition and growth in the number of products in most markets in the last ten to twenty years has meant that consumers have higher expectations of the goods they buy. So they are less easily influenced than before by advertising and promotions. This is forcing firms to move away from 'push' approaches towards 'pull' – where the transaction is seen as a process in which both parties benefit equally. To develop effective 'pull' strategies, firms are finding that they have to achieve a deeper understanding of consumer behaviour than was necessary with a 'push' approach.

A model of the buying process

There are several models of the buying process and most of them include the following five steps – identification of a need, search for ways to satisfy the need, evaluation of alternatives, making the buying decision, and post-purchase feelings. Obviously not every consumer goes logically through all these stages each time they buy something and the lower the price of a product, the more simple the buying process is likely to be. However, it may be useful for a firm to compare its marketing approach to the model to ensure that its message can influence all five stages. Often companies neglect one or two of the stages. Most commonly it is the last stage – post-purchase feelings. Whenever a consumer has made a major purchase, he will be more sensitive to the advertising of competitive products and will compare the reality of what he has bought to the advertised benefits of other offerings. Usually he will feel some unease about whether he has made the right decision. If the firm reduces the consumer doubt by providing clear instructions, good after-sales support, training and technical help, interest in the customer and so on, the consumer is likely to recommend the product to others. If the company neglects this stage, its customers will tend to be reticent about proposing its products.

A model of the selling process

Just as there are many models of the buying process, there are also a number of selling formulas. One is AIDDA, which stands for attention, interest, desire, decision, action. The significance of a formula like AIDDA is that it is important to go through each step if the sale is to be successful – unless you have a person's attention and then interest, you cannot expect to be able to motivate them to take the action you want. Too often when firms want to sell a new product or people want to sell a proposal, they become blinded by the benefits they believe they can offer and forget to ensure that they have first stimulated their target's attention and interest.

Four types of purchase

One theory proposes that there are four main types of purchase decision – complex, habitual, variety-seeking and high price commodity. A complex decision occurs when the item is a high value item and there are a number of differentiated products to choose from (cars, houses). A high price commodity decision refers to items like televisions and carpets, where the product is bought infrequently, is expensive and there are many similar or indistinguishable offerings available. Most products are bought as habitual decisions – normally these are low value items where consumers maintain brand loyalty either out of habit or because of better availability of the product. A variety-seeking decision is when a consumer becomes bored with the usual brand and decides to experiment with competitive products.

The level of involvement of the consumer and type of buying decision will have a major effect on a firm's marketing approach. For example, if it is a high price, high involvement item and a product is market leader, then the marketing should reinforce the buyer's perception of the product as being the best item available. But if the product is not dominant, then the marketing should be aimed at reducing the level of risk a buyer will feel if he strays from the generally accepted first choice – this may call for offering better service, 'money back if not satisfied' guarantee, or some other additional benefit. Likewise with the lower price, lower involvement decision, the market leader will try to encourage loyalty, while the challengers will want to move people towards variety-seeking behaviour.

Customer motivation

Every product is just a physical item when it leaves the factory. But it becomes a complex collection of real and perceived benefits when bought by the consumer.

People purchase products and services for many different reasons – a product's functions, its perceived value, the person's self-image, the availability of the product or service, for convenience or self-improvement, or whatever. Usually the reason includes a mixture of most of the above.

Good marketing is based on understanding consumer behaviour

In deciding a marketing approach, it is important to be aware of the multiplicity of factors which motivate the purchaser. It is easy for a marketer to list a product or service's features. But successful marketing requires that he links these in to the drives of the purchaser, in order to provide a series of benefits the purchaser can relate to. Canon, for example, came from nowhere to be a major competitor in the photocopier market. They achieved this by identifying that, while other firms offered expensive high performance machines, secretaries wanted smaller, simpler models they could have in their own offices, rather than having to stand in a queue to use a centrally-located machine. Canon satisfied a need rather than just offering performance and features.

Decision-making unit

Another factor which needs to be taken into account when considering consumer behaviour is the nature of the group who decides what product is bought – the decision-making unit (DMU). Depending on the type of purchase, its cost and the level of buyer involvement, this can vary from one to several people. One model identifies five potential roles in a DMU: initiator, influencer, decider, purchaser and user. The initiator signals the need for the purchase, the influencer (often a friend or family member) may have experience of a product and so makes a recommendation, the decider has the final say, the purchaser will conduct the transaction and the product will be given to the user. Changes in life-style – more single-parent families, a growth in affluent older people, an increase in working mothers – have made significant changes in the DMU, which firms must be aware of if they are to send the right messages to potential buyers.

Dissatisfied customers

A series of studies on consumer behaviour suggested that up to 96 per cent of dissatisfied customers do not complain and of these 91 per cent do not come back to that manufacturer's products.[11] Moreover, the average dissatisfied customer tells ten people of his disappointment with the product or service. So companies are only fooling themselves and others when they point to a low level of complaints as proof of customer satisfaction. Normally when they survey customers, they will receive quite a different picture. There is thus a need for firms not to sit back in contentment at few complaints, but to actively go out and question customers regarding how they felt about their purchases. For example, did they live up to expectations? If not why not? Was the price right? Would they buy the product again or recommend it?

The study also showed that of the customers who complained, 62 per cent came back if they felt their complaints were resolved and 90 per cent came back if they believed their complaints were resolved quickly. This suggests that complaints departments might better serve their employers if they put customer service first and did not fall into the usual trap of assuming that the company can do no wrong and that all complaints are to be fobbed off rather than seriously looked at.

32
Setting prices

Price and cost

Often companies assume that there should be a direct relationship between price and cost. They calculate the cost of making a product or providing a service and then arrive at a price by adding on a certain standard mark-up. Yet the idea of fixed prices for products is very much a part of twentieth-century Western culture and was spread largely through the growth of nationwide store chains. Any visitor to the Third World will know that prices are flexible and subject to negotiation. A shopkeeper in Delhi or Bangkok uses the cost of the product as the floor, below which he will try not to go. But then he attempts to set a price, above this level, dependent on his estimation of the buyer's willingness and ability to pay. He is in effect pricing according to his own needs and the value of the item to the customer.

Price is in fact, like advertising and product features, just one of the elements of the marketing mix. It should thus be just as flexible as design or advertising budget. But too often it is treated as a fixed aspect of the product. The cost of a product determines whether or not you enter a market, by giving you a base below which you cannot profitably go. But the actual price you could charge will then depend on the marketing strategy you adopt and not just be made up of the cost plus a standard mark-up.

Pricing strategies

There are six main strategies a firm can adopt, each of which will cause a quite different price to be set.

Market penetration

The firm may have built a large production facility to serve a market and need high volumes to utilize their capacity and recover their investment. In this case it will tend to set a very competitive, low price to generate high sales.

Market skimming

If a company has limited production capacity which it feels it can easily sell, it will set a high price so that it only sells its limited volume to those customers who are prepared to pay well for the product. When this high price segment is saturated, the firm may slightly lower its price to attract the next group of customers. Pocket calculators, for example, were first sold at high prices to scientists and businessmen. Gradually as the price dropped, more and more groups (students, general consumers and schoolchildren) felt it was worth buying one.

Cost orientation

As discussed, some firms set prices by calculating their production costs and adding a mark-up. This method can go badly wrong if it is difficult to allocate costs to, for example, small versus large orders or to one product size versus another. Usually changes in machines, methods or product mix mean that some costs have to be allocated by the costing department in a way that may not accurately represent how costs are driven. This can cause a situation where prices do not reflect the actual costs, and where prices influence market demand in a way which is not in the interests of the firm's profitability.

Price discrimination

The firm identifies that different segments of the market have different expectations of the product and will pay different prices. Here, rather like the Delhi shopkeeper, price will be varied according to the customer's willingness to pay. This is most common in travel, for example in having six or seven different fares for the same flight or in offering off-peak prices on public transport or holidays. Rather than viewing the off-peak as a price reduction, one could see the 'normal' fare as a penalty put on a captive market of travellers who have to use the service at certain times. Firms making products can also price-discriminate, for example, by making minor cosmetic changes in a product and then offering, at different price levels – the 'professional's' model, the 'home' model, the 'student's' model and so on.

Survival

In a market which is declining or where there is overcapacity, a firm may want to sit it out until the market grows again or some competitors withdraw. Here the firm will want to cover variable costs (materials, labour, energy) and possibly obtain some contribution to fixed costs (to pay off loans and to fund capital investments). However it may be prepared to price at or below total costs in order to survive.

Experience/Learning curve

According to the learning curve, the greater volume a company makes of a product, the lower will be its costs. This is due to the fact that the more experience it gains in purchasing, manufacturing, marketing and distribution, the more it will be able to find new methods or materials and learn from early mistakes. Also there are many one-off setting-up costs, which will not be repeated. Rather than setting a price using cost price plus margin, a firm can anticipate the benefits of the learning curve and possibly price lower than rivals, in the knowledge that as volume grows its costs will reduce to a level where the lower price will become profitable.

Price elasticity of demand

This can be a major influence on a firm's pricing. A product is said to have elastic demand if a certain percentage increase or reduction in price will cause a greater increase or reduction in sales. It has inelastic demand if a certain percentage change in price causes a smaller percentage change in demand. Products, like washing powder, which are all very similar tend to have elastic demand as a small price reduction in one brand may encourage consumers to switch from more expensive brands to cheaper ones. Luxury items, like expensive cars, perfumes, furs, will normally have inelastic demand as raising the price has very little effect on the level of sales.

If your product has elastic demand it may pay to reduce price to generate extra volume, though if competitors will match your move, then you will both end up losing. Whereas if your product's demand is inelastic, you can probably raise prices with little or no effect on demand. Advertising and creating differential advantage are ways of building consumer loyalty to a brand to reduce its price elasticity and thus protect it from the effects of competitors lowering their prices.

Common mistakes

Some of the mistakes firms most frequently make when setting prices include:

- Not updating cost-plus-margin prices to reflect changes in machines, methods, materials, product mix, the learning curve and other cost factors. When cost plus pricing does not accurately represent costs, demand may be skewed towards products and order sizes which have lower margins, because their prices do not fully reflect costs.
- Not changing prices often enough to benefit from changes in the market. For example, if new, lower price segments are added to a market, a firm should either reduce price to capture some volume from this segment or else issue a 'special' or 'economy' model specifically targeted at the new segment.
- Not understanding the cost advantages of becoming a brand leader and maintaining a price structure which leaves a firm in the disadvantageous position of being number two, three or four in a market.
- Being inflexible in negotiating with retailers and forgetting that many customers use shop displays as their shopping list and will not search out your product if it is not readily available. It thus may be worth achieving distribution at almost any price, as the volume generated can at least make some contribution to your fixed costs.

Summary

Your costs may set a floor for your price, the sustainability of your differential advantage can fix a ceiling, and the prices of competitors' products and substitutes may provide a reference point. But finally, as with the shopkeeper in Delhi or Bangkok, your decision on price should be a function of your needs, capabilities and strategy and your estimation of your customers' willingness and ability to pay.

33
Marketing and the product life cycle

Product life cycle (PLC) and customer needs

Any product exists to satisfy a customer need (food, transport, entertainment) and any firm's product is only one possible way of satisfying a need. Eventually a new or better way of satisfying the need will be developed and demand for a firm's product will decline. This process has led to the idea of the PLC – that any product will only satisfy a customer need for a limited period and will generally go through the stages of being introduced, growth in demand, levelling off and then decline in demand. The reason why many firms are caught out and affected by the maturity or decline of their products is that they have come to see themselves as the makers of a certain product, rather than the satisfiers of a certain need and so fail to think ahead to new ways of satisfying that need. For example, in Europe and America railway companies saw air travel as a competitor. What they should have perceived, was that they were in the transportation business, not just the railway business. Had they realized this, they would have used their experience in transportation to expand into air transport instead of, as in America, being virtually destroyed by it. The railways did not understand that they were only one way of satisfying people's need for transport. Likewise, the Hollywood film studios first saw television as a threat and would not cooperate with the TV companies. Only when they switched their focus from making films to satisfying the need for entertainment, did they exploit the opportunities television offered. After the oil crisis of the 1970s the oil companies, on the other hand, realized that oil was only one possible answer to

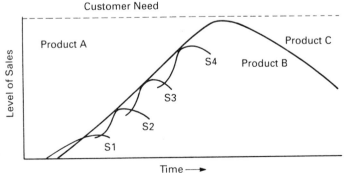

Figure 11

people's need for energy and several quickly diversified by buying coal and other energy sources.

The figure opposite shows one model of the PLC. This model makes two key points:

1. Basic needs are fairly constant – the areas Product A, B and C are intended to show how three different products successively satisfy the customer need. If the need was entertainment, the three sectors could be radio, cinema then television. If the need was taking photographs, the three areas could be basic 35 mm cameras, SLR cameras and then video cameras.

2. Markets do not grow, they add segments – it is misleading just to think of a market growing because this gives the idea of more and more similar buyers entering a market. Such a view suggests that a firm can continue to offer a basic product. What happens in most markets is that new types of consumer (new segments) enter the market. These new segments are shown by the curves S1, S2, S3 and so on. This means that a marketer constantly has to adapt his offering to appeal to these new segments. For example, calculators were probably first bought by scientists, engineers and accountants, next general businessmen entered the market, then students, ordinary consumers and schoolchildren. All these segments each required a different type of calculator. Some manufacturers remained in the first segment by offering ever more complex and powerful models – by becoming product- rather than market-driven, they restricted themselves to a small section of the market. Other makers recognized the new segments and brought out product variations to suit each new group of consumers. Moreover, by moving to the new segments and increasing volume, they were able to generate cost advantages, which allowed them to go back into the first segments and outcompete the firms who had tried to restrict themselves to serving specialists.

'Creative destruction' and positioning

This model of the PLC has two crucial implications for firms. Firstly, they must always try and look beyond the product they make to the needs the products satisfy. If they tie themselves too closely to the product, they will decline when it does. This has prompted the idea of 'creative destruction' – all products will eventually become obsolete, so rather than allowing a competitor to benefit from a product's demise, a firm should itself constantly search for the technology or item which will replace its best-selling models.

Secondly, a firm must continuously analyse its markets to identify any new customer segments and either reposition its existing products or issue new variations to target these new segments and serve them better than competitors.

Stages of the PLC

Introduction

Here the product is new and is usually at a fairly basic stage of its development. There are few, if any, competitors making a similar product – the main competition is the type of product the new product is replacing. The marketing issue is to sell the concept – to make customers believe their needs can better be satisfied by the new offering than by the product they are used to. The volume produced is usually low and prices high. The first firm into the market has an excellent opportunity to dominate it, though often it becomes too product-oriented and fails to adapt to new market segments.

Depending on several factors such as how aware the market is, the firm's own production capacity, how close competitors are and how strongly the previous technology can defend itself, a company can choose to introduce the product slowly at a high price or else go for high volume quickly at a lower price level.

Growth

Once the product has gained acceptance, growth in sales may be rapid. Other firms, seeing the opportunity to make attractive profits, will enter the market. This will tend to push prices down, especially if (as in the personal computer market) the arrival of new competitors creates over-capacity. The fall in prices will also be fuelled by cost reductions due to higher volumes and the effects of the experience curve. The drop in prices will probably encourage new groups of people to buy the product and so new segments will be added to the market.

Firms will move away from selling the concept to selling their particular brand. They will add styling, quality and extra features to distinguish their offering from those of competitors. There will also be a tendency to move to new distribution channels to reach the new market segments better. The firm which manages to dominate the market at this stage will probably emerge as the most profitable, when the long maturity phase is reached. Many companies are lulled into a false sense of security by the growth stage. They see sales rising and assume profitability will follow naturally. But the most far-sighted companies will monitor market share, rather than growth rate, because they realize that when market growth slows, only the top brands will retain profitability.

Maturity

This is the longest phase of the PLC, so most marketing work will be with products in mature markets. This phase tends to be marked by price and advertising wars – competitors have invested in large mass production facilities and the only way they can increase sales and profitability is by taking market share from other competitors, as the market has ceased growing. Often there is a 'shakeout' as price and advertising wars force all but the strongest few brands out of the market. The situation is exacerbated by the power of larger retailers to negotiate low prices, as they can decide which of the competing brands will be stocked. Further pressure is added when retailers produce their own lower price brands, so there is often only room on the shelves for the retailer's brand and one other competitor, usually the brand leader.

To maintain profitability in maturity, you either have to be brand leader or else build up layers of differential advantage around your product so that consumers can distinguish it from competitors and so that stockists see benefits in carrying it. You can also try to become the lowest cost, lowest price producer, but this puts you in a vulnerable position if competitors feel pressurized to lower their prices to gain sales volume.

In a growth market advertising plays an important role in giving each brand its distinctive image. However, in the maturity phase these images are fairly well established and difficult to change. Marketing expenditure tends therefore to move away from above-the-line activity (advertising) to below-the-line (sales promotion) as marketers try to tempt consumers to switch brands. Advertising agencies often try to resist this shift, as it is not in their interest. When they succeed with this, they can often convince their clients to spend large sums on advertising which is largely ineffective.

Decline

As the market begins to shrink, some competitors may start to withdraw, while others, perhaps because they are dependent on the market, will hang on in the hope that better times will come. Innovative companies will look for ways to upgrade the product to satisfy customer needs better or even move over to the next generation of products. Profits do not need to be low during the decline stage, especially if other competitors are leaving the market. Most companies with products in the decline stage will try to cut costs, reduce advertising and promotion and reduce the product range. Decline can be reversed for a considerable period of time by repositioning. Consumer tastes and trends tend to go in cycles and sometimes older products can be dressed up to take advantage of a change in consumer taste. Many 'traditional' food products, for example, got new leases of life as buyers turned away from modern, processed foods.

Main criticisms of PLC models

Critics of the theory of PLCs have claimed:

- It encourages managers in mature or declining markets to give up and withdraw (as Western companies have done in the face of Japanese competition) rather than look for innovative turnaround strategies.
- It can become a self-fulfilling prophecy – if you believe a product is declining and you withhold investment, it will inevitably decline.
- Life cycles for different products are so varied that the model is of little practical use.
- It causes many firms to adopt similar strategies.
- Products may appear to be mature, when in fact small changes in features or a minor repositioning can start a new phase of growth by attracting increased usage or more segments.

In spite of these criticisms, the PLC is a powerful tool for helping firms see the need to focus on customer needs, rather than products, for showing the importance of repositioning to target new segments and for giving a background against which to develop marketing strategies.

34
Industrial marketing

The buying decision

Theoretically an industrial buyer has one over-riding concern – how to help his organization make more money. Therefore, the key for a seller to an industrial buyer is not simply to offer the lowest price or the best service, or the highest quality. Rather it is to try and express whatever advantage your product has in terms of the buyer's goal – making more profit. Therefore you must try and understand a buyer's operating cost structure and how your product or service will affect it. For example, if you supply some item which accounts for 10 per cent of an industry's costs, and you can supply it 10 per cent cheaper than a competitor, or with 10 per cent less waste, or with a 10 per cent longer operating life, you have two ways of communicating this. Either you can talk of the 10 per cent difference, or else you can show that your product will add 1 per cent to your customer's profitability. Although it may not sound like much, if your customer is working on a net profit of 5–6 per cent, by buying your product he can increase his profitability to 6–7 per cent (a 17–20 per cent increase). Probably the second way of expressing your product's advantage would be the most effective.

In fact, an industrial buyer will have many reasons for preferring one product over another. But the example above does underline the importance of identifying the buyer's objectives and relating your product's advantages directly to these, instead of just stressing your product's distinctive features.

Risk often plays a key role in an industrial buying decision. The buyer's reputation, and possibly job, is put at risk with each major purchase he makes. He is unlikely to put himself at risk just because you offer a slightly lower price. However, he will often be willing to pay a little more if he believes you can significantly reduce the risk involved in the purchase by giving better service, operator training, guaranteed delivery date, helping him justify the purchase to his superiors or whatever. Sales reps have a tendency to believe that price is the deciding factor in most purchases and will push to be able to offer the most competitive price. But they can frequently be more successful when they try to put together a package of benefits which provide a reasonable price level and also reduce the buyer's perception of risk. This avoidance of risk is nicely expressed in the well-known expression 'nobody ever got fired for buying an IBM'. In fact, IBM are frequently accused of playing on buyers' fears of making the wrong decision by using a FUD (fear, uncertainty and doubt) marketing approach – every time a competitor announces a better product than its IBM equivalent, IBM, it is said, start to spread rumours that they will soon launch a superior product, causing buyers to wait for IBM's product rather than taking the risk of moving to a less well-known supplier.

Economic value to the customer (EVC)

The concept of Economic Value to the Customer (EVC) is used to express the idea that an item can have quite different values for different customers. If you supply a product with strong technical support, this can be more valuable to a small customer with limited technical resources than to a large firm. Or if you can offer just-in-time delivery, this will be most interesting to a firm which is trying to reduce its stock levels. When marketing a product, you should first target those customers for whom the EVC is highest. Moreover, the EVC should be a major influence on the price you ask. So with any product you should try to make some estimate of the EVC. For example, it may save so many maintenance hours and hours of lost production per year, or it may have a higher yield, higher resale value, or lower defect rate – all these kinds of advantage should be calculated for each customer and used as part of your marketing process.

Decision-making unit (DMU)

Depending on how large a purchase is, the decision-making unit in industrial marketing can be quite complex. One model suggests the DMU can consist of six groups of people: users, influencers, deciders, approvers, buyers and gate-keepers. (Gate-keepers are those who can control access to key members of the DMU – they could range from secretaries who can help you make appointments, to any person in the organization who has the power to filter the information a marketer wishes to present to the DMU.)

The different members of the DMU will usually have quite different backgrounds and objectives: a buyer may want to work with a supplier he knows well, a technical specialist may look for certain performance characteristics, the approver (financial controller) might focus on short-term capital requirements rather than estimates of total yield over the product's life, an influencer may have bought a similar item and feel a need to justify his earlier decision by recommending the same supplier, and so on. It is difficult, but important, to try and identify who is in the DMU and their interests, loyalties and power over the decision. Although the industrial buying process is generally more rational than a consumer purchase, with major purchases it can be strongly biased by political power and so the marketer has to identify what factors will be considered crucial by those who yield this power.

Features of the industrial market

There are fewer buyers in industrial markets, compared to consumer markets. They are larger, more concentrated and usually more rational. Also relationships between buyers and sellers in industrial markets tend to be based on personal contact, are close and can last for a considerable period of time.

Demand in industrial markets is often quite different from consumer demand. Industrial market demand is called 'derived' demand as it is dependent on the demand for some finished good. It thus cannot be so easily directly influenced by a seller, who, for example, wants to increase volume by lowering price. A small increase in consumer demand can often have little or no effect on industrial demand as it can be absorbed with existing production facilities. But a growth in consumer demand above a certain point can cause a much larger increase in industrial demand as several firms may decide to increase capacity at the same time. Similarly a small decrease in consumer demand can have a much larger effect on industrial demand as firms in an industry postpone investment and try to cut down stock levels.

Trends in industrial buying

The most significant trend in industrial buying is a move away from the practice of buying mainly on the basis of price and switching suppliers when a cheaper bid was received. Instead firms are tending to give much more weight to factors such as reliability, quality and delivery performance and are trying to consolidate their buying with fewer suppliers, to whom they are giving longer-term contracts. This change has been strongly influenced by the ideas of just-in-time deliveries and zero defects.

Another trend is a tendency for buyers to want total solutions or systems as opposed to components, materials or machines. Many companies can no longer afford the time or resources to devote to deciding how a material can best be used, a machine can be serviced, operators can be trained or a service should be performed. So the supplier who offers a total package which answers most aspects of an issue will tend to be preferred, even if he does not offer the lowest price.

These two trends have important implications for marketers. They should move from offering individual items to providing a total service package or solution, they should fight harder to obtain contracts as these will tend to be for longer periods, and they should try to establish a mutually advantageous relationship with customers which can even turn into a kind of partnership. The most advanced marketers are linking in their computer systems to those of customers to permit direct ordering, are setting up joint development programmes with customers and are encouraging contacts at numerous levels to aid communication, problem solving and relationship building. It is probably more difficult to cause an industrial buyer to shift to a new supplier, than it is to have a consumer change brands. It is therefore crucial for the industrial marketer to take a long-term view – to try to start a relationship with buyers rather than looking for quick profits.

35
Marketing services

Product versus service marketing

There are a number of distinctive features of services like hotels, insurance companies, banks, airlines, private hospitals and restaurants, which make the task of marketing them quite different from that of product marketing. Some of the most important are as follows:

Services are intangible

Products are high in what are called 'search qualities' – physical features a potential buyer can examine before making the purchase decision. However, services are more difficult to judge until they are actually purchased. Some services provided by experts (lawyers, doctors, car mechanics) may not be able to be judged even after purchase as the buyer lacks the expertise to evaluate what he has received. So while product advertising tends to try to add something intangible (style, quality, physical attractiveness, family happiness) to mundane items like prepared foods, clothes, cars or perfume, service advertising often attempts to give some physical substance to the intangible – banks and insurance companies are represented by eagles, rocks, umbrellas or horses, hotels and restaurants give their staff uniforms, and private hospitals feature their patients being treated by the most modern machinery available.

Services cannot be stored

Most services are produced and consumed either simultaneously (insurance, flights, medical attention) or within a short time of being purchased (most meals, hopefully). Because they cannot be stored, a key marketing task for services is to utilize capacity by trying to balance supply and demand. With transport, for example, off-peak and off-season pricing is an attempt to lure people to use the service at less busy periods. Hotels often offer weekend rates to fill rooms when there are few businessmen staying and restaurants offer 'happy hours' to drum up custom during quiet periods.

Another way of matching supply and demand is to be able to vary supply. This can be done by having a number of part-time staff (restaurants, hotels), by dividing up the work so that non-essential activities (stocking shelves, stock checks) are done during low volume periods, by training staff to do several different jobs so they are flexible and can adapt to the level of demand, and by using machines instead of people (banks, car washes, canteens) to provide the service.

Quality is variable

While the quality of most products is fairly standardized and controlled at the factory, the quality of many services depends largely on the person who delivers them and the relationship that person has with the customer. So the success of a service is often less in the hands of managers than it is of the lowest paid person in the organization – the receptionist, cleaner, waiter, airline steward, cashier – who has most customer contact.

The issue of how to motivate the person who provides the service to maintain constant high quality is one of the most crucial in marketing the service and the one where many organizations are most noticeably unsuccessful. There is little that enrages a customer more than to waste hours in a dirty, overcrowded airport lounge with no information and even less service by an airline that has spent millions on a campaign boasting it is dedicated to its passengers or to be constantly messed around by incompetent staff in a bank that constantly advertises its devotion to customer service.

One way to try and standardize the quality of service is to reduce customer contact and move as much of the service provision as possible to machines or to 'backroom' people – advertising agencies will limit customer contact to one or two key individuals, banks and building societies have automatic tellers. Another method is to make the customer do a certain amount of the work – restaurants where the client chooses or even cooks his own meal, holidays where people plan their own routes. Also organizations will attempt to manage customers' perceptions through advertising or the design of the environment, so that even if the service is variable in quality, customers may still have the impression of having received value.

But most often organizations try to deal with the problem of variable quality of service delivery through internal marketing campaigns. 'Internal marketing' consists of applying the techniques of customer marketing to an organization's staff so that they value the organization and feel it is important to perform their job well. Internal marketing can range from training courses, presentations to staff and best service awards to efforts to redesign job and working conditions to suit and motivate employees better. Internal marketing recognizes that a service's most vulnerable point is the area of customer contact and tries to guard against deficiencies by selling the idea of service to staff.

Services are easily copied

Copying a product may be expensive as it can require large capital investment in production facilities. But any new feature that any service introduces (new types of bank account, telephones in planes, free offers to frequent users) can usually be easily copied. So achieving differentiation may be much more difficult for a service than a product. Either a service must constantly innovate new offerings, which will be quickly copied, to try and stay ahead, or else it can hope to achieve differentiation by constantly providing a higher standard of quality than competitors can match through the motivation and abilities of its people. Some of the most successful service companies have worked on the principle that competitiveness starts and ends at the job interview – the firm which attracts the best people will tend to provide the best service.

Blueprinting

One method for identifying ways of improving the marketing of services has been called 'blueprinting'. This consists of drawing a flow chart identifying every stage of the preparation and delivery of a service. Next the line of visibility (those aspects the customer will see) is highlighted. Then a number of questions should be answered:

- Can the degree of customer contact be reduced to help standardize the quality of delivery
- What are the potential 'fail points'? How can these be made less vulnerable?
- Do the concept and method of delivery reinforce each other? For example, is the location consistent with the service? Do the physical surroundings enhance or detract from the service quality? Is staff training and motivation enough to ensure delivery is satisfactory?
- Is there a fast enough turnround of customers and sufficiently high utilization of customers?
- Are there busy or low periods? What is the best way to cope with these? Are there sufficient staff to deal with busy periods?
- Do staff know exactly what is expected of them?
- Is the balance between efficiency and service quality correct?
- Is the advertising of the service consistent with its delivery or will customers be disappointed?

Because a service is so dependent on the people who deliver it and the location in which it is delivered, service marketing can seem to be a wider concept than product marketing. Service marketing necessarily includes designing the whole process of delivery as well as its advertising and promotion.

36
Writing a marketing plan

Traditionally, writing a marketing plan has been seen as being purely the prerogative of the marketing department. Normally they prepare the plan, submit it to top management for approval and then implement whatever course of action is finally agreed. In many firms the production department, purchasing, product development and finance often either don't ever see the marketing plan or else only receive a copy once it is a fait accompli. This practice is based on a view of the firm as a series of almost independent activities of which the last is the function of marketing and it overlooks the importance of integrating all the parts of the supply chain.

But if the firm is seen as a sequence of closely related functions whose sole purpose is to supply value to the customer more effectively than competitors, then the idea of the marketing plan belonging solely to marketing is inadequate.

Role of the marketing plan

Assuming that the firm is marketing-oriented, as opposed to being production-, sales- or product-oriented, then the satisfaction of customer needs must be the driving force for the whole organization. If this is the case, then the marketing plan is not just one isolated function's forward view. Rather, it is a description of the way the whole organization will do business and thus is the base to which all other functions should relate their activities. Therefore, though the promotional and advertising aspects of the plan may be left to the marketing department, the basic decisions on the nature of the product, its price, the customer targets, the choice of distribution and all new product development are issues for the whole organization and not just marketing.

Too many companies fail to understand the importance of linking all activities to the marketing strategy and end up with a series of disjointed departments often in a state of conflict with each other. This can be partially overcome by making the development of marketing strategy the responsibility of a cross-functional group representing all key departments. In this way all departments have participated in deciding the marketing approach and have 'ownership' of it. They thus will have a fuller understanding of their part in successfully implementing the firm's marketing strategy.

Structure and contents

Although there are several different ways a marketing plan can be structured, it is generally accepted it should contain most of the following:

Executive summary

This should give a brief review of the product's position in its market and the firm's marketing strategy. There should also be an overview of the next year's marketing plan, its costs and expected results, the likely competitive reaction and how this will be dealt with. The aim is that people reading the plan can quickly grasp the logical connection between market situation, strategy, plan and results. It is important, even at this stage to show awareness of competitors and their probable strategies. Too often marketing plans are written as if in a kind of vacuum with insufficient consideration given to how the competition will behave and the effects of this on the firm.

Marketing strategy

It can be useful to start off the main section of the report with a statement of the firm's basic marketing strategy. This could cover such items as the type of products produced, the target market(s), the price level and reason for this, the customer needs which the products satisfy and the stage of the product in the product life-cycle. Additionally, readers' perspective on the situation may be broadened by a brief discussion of how the customer need, at which the products are aimed, will be satisfied over the next five, ten and fifteen years and what the firm is doing to upgrade its products, so they are not displaced by a better method of satisfying the customer need.

This is the section of the report which, more than any other, should be produced by an inter-departmental team as it is the basis to which all the firm's activities should be linked.

Current market situation

This should include data about the size of the market, its history, details of the major competitors, analysis of their strategies, market share and profitability information, a description of the distribution system and an analysis of the market's position in the overall macroeconomic environment.

Of key importance in this part is the need to trace trends in the market's development, competitors' and consumers' behaviour and the general economic situation, and to explain what implications these trends have for the firm, its products and its marketing approach. A common mistake is to produce an impressive mass of data without interpreting it.

As appendices to this part, product profiles (comparing a firm's products to those of competitors against a number of key criteria) could help readers better visualize a firm's current market situation.

Marketing options

Through using a tool like a SWOT analysis (see Chapter 21, SWOT Analysis) the report can quickly highlight the firm's main strengths and weaknesses, what the major threats are and what options are open to it. A frequent weakness of marketing plans is that they may contain a detailed consideration of one single marketing choice, but they fail to examine other available choices and to explain why these other possible choices were rejected.

Some examples of the types of option a firm might consider are increasing market share through lower prices, higher advertising, improved product features, heavy promotional activity and so on. Or else a firm may decide to increase sales revenue through maintaining market share, increasing sales price and strengthening differential advantage to justify the higher price. Alternatively revenue can be increased by encouraging greater usage, expansion abroad, licensing abroad or bringing new user segments into the market.

Objectives

Whatever marketing approach is chosen, this needs to be expressed both in terms of clear and measurable marketing objectives and financial objectives. The marketing objectives may include planned market shares, level of consumer awareness, consumer rating against competitive products, price levels and number of distribution outlets. Financial objectives will consist of expected sales revenue, profit levels, return on investment and marketing spend.

Marketing programme

The marketing programme covers all the activities which will take place over the period of the marketing plan – advertising campaigns, sales promotion, trade promotions, marketing and advertising research, and any new product development. The programme should contain time-frames, responsibilities and costs. It should also detail how the implementation will be monitored and controlled – what the milestones will be, how achievement will be measured, how often it will be measured and what kinds of contingency plans there are if performance falls behind plan. In particular, attention should be given to thinking through what competitors' marketing programmes are likely to be and how these will affect the firm's chances of achieving its own marketing objectives.

Profit and loss statement

The report should conclude with a profit and loss statement for the next year. If major investments are planned in marketing, for example a new product launch, or elsewhere, it may be necessary also to include a cash flow projection. This will allow the firm to identify any possible liquidity problems arising from the investment and so it can take preventive action ahead of the problem occurring.

CREATIVE PROBLEM-SOLVING

37 Creative thinking

38 Brainstorming

39 Problem-solving

40 Mind-mapping

41 Quality circles

42 Other creative-thinking techniques

37
Creative thinking

The more research is done into the brain, the more we learn about its vast potential, rather than its limitations. Yet many of us do not get the chance to or choose not to develop the brain's enormous potential. Some common excuses we use are our age – 'I can't remember things, I must be getting old'; our position in an organization – 'how am I meant to know, nobody tells me anything'; and our humanity – 'I'm sorry I must have forgotten, after all I'm only human'. But none of these really stands up to closer scrutiny. Common belief is that our mental powers decline with age. However, the older we are, the greater is the store of knowledge and experiences we have to build on. Most school classes start with half the children having forgotten books, pens, ink, pencils and so on. A class of university students or adults simply does not have the same problem. Though it may be true that we design organizations which keep many people in the dark much of the time, such information control is a matter of choice rather than inevitability. There are better and more open ways of working together which we can adopt, if we have the strength to break away from traditional ways of operating. And as for only being human, we normally use so little of our brain's potential that this excuse just cannot hold water.

By understanding a little more about how the brain works, we can significantly increase the effectiveness with which we use it.

Creative and analytical thinking

It is generally recognized that there are two main types of thinking. These have been called analytical and creative, convergent and divergent, or vertical and lateral. Any thought will normally not be either totally creative or completely analytical. But it will tend towards one or other of these opposites.

The table opposite lists some of the key differences between analytical and creative thinking:

ANALYTICAL THINKING	CREATIVE THINKING
Looks for 'one' correct answer	Tries to generate many possible solutions
Proceeds by logical steps	Jumps freely from one idea to another
Selects and evaluates ideas	Does not judge ideas
Adult – based on discipline and self-control	Child-like – allows fantasy and imagination
Builds on analysis of information	Finds new connections between existing information
Serious, hard work	Fun, enthusiasm, humour

In general, it can be said that analytical thinking assumes there is one correct answer to a problem and tries to converge on it through a grown-up, logical, disciplined approach of information analysis leading to firmly-based conclusions. Creative thinking, on the other hand, is divergent in that it tries to burst out from a problem to generate as many ideas as possible, however ridiculous they may seem at first. Moreover, there is no need for the ideas to be logically connected or based on hard evidence. Creative thinking has sometimes been compared to telling a joke, because the discovery of new links between existing pieces of information can be like revealing an unexpected punch-line. Most people are experienced in analytical thinking, but have had little chance or encouragement to think creatively and so have not really developed an important side of their personality.

A common method of showing the limitations of analytical compared to creative thinking is to ask a group of people to think of as many uses of a paperclip as they can. Normally there are twenty to thirty ideas. Then you change the situation round completely and ask them to think of things which you could not use a paperclip for. Of course, there aren't that many. This quickly highlights how people's logical, analytical approach to the first question prevented them seeing the rich variety of solutions to the problem.

Education and creative thinking

We are all born with the ability to think creatively. In fact, in our early years, we are often better at creative than at analytical thinking. However, when, as young children, we would play or make up stories, most of us were constantly told to stop being ridiculous and childish. We were given to understand that it is adult to be realistic and factual, and to exercise discipline and self-control. We were discouraged from showing our feelings and learnt how to repress them. However, we were also being made to repress our creativity.

Unless we were very lucky, our whole education was based on a classical model, which emphasized the importance of logic rather than creativity. We were taught Latin, mathematics, physics, even Greek, but not about how the brain works and how to improve our ways of thinking. In some subjects, such as mathematics, we were told that even if we did not get the right answers, we could do well by showing we had used a logical, reasoned way of arriving at our answer. Our schooling encouraged the belief in the supremacy of logical analysis, as this is easier to teach and to test in exams, than creative thinking. Moreover, much of our education consisted of learning lists of facts off by heart, rather than being taught how best to use knowledge.

This suppression of the creative side of our nature was reinforced by the way most schools used tests, examinations and IQ tests to rate our abilities and place us in relation to each other. The practice of giving us marks, specific levels and even putting us in streams, based on our 'scientifically proven' abilities, implied a kind of rigidity – as if we would always be fixed at a certain level and could never really improve, except perhaps through intensive study. Grading us was in a way a denial of the importance of creativity.

Barriers to creative thinking

Partly due to our upbringing and education, most of us are prevented from thinking creatively by a number of psychological barriers. The most common are:

Patterns, recipes and repertoires

A key function of the brain is to identify familiar patterns, when we are bombarded by a mass of information. One model talks of us all developing our own recipes and repertoires. Recipes are ways we have learnt to think and judge situations. Repertoires are collections of recipes. As we have new experiences we gradually change our repertoires by abandoning old, outdated recipes and replacing them with new ones. Without this ability to recognize patterns and accumulate a stock of interpretative mechanisms, we could not survive. However, it can also limit our creativity by causing us to seek out what seems familiar and act in ways which we know have been successful in the past.

Both individuals and organizations develop recipes and repertoires. Accountants, marketers, engineers will all tend to view a particular situation in their own particular ways, due to their own experiences, backgrounds and interests. Likewise organizations may react to an event in almost predictable ways, because of their individual cultures – for example, some will tend to see cost-cutting and control as a way of dealing with problems, while others may favour innovation and growth. The disadvantage is that our recipes and repertoires often prevent us considering new ways of thinking and acting.

Evaluation and judgement

When faced with new ideas, we have a tendency to evaluate and condemn them, before looking for their strong points. 'Yes, but the problem is . . .' is a fairly common reaction to other people's suggestions. And the more we shoot other people's ideas down in flames, the more they will treat ours the same way, and the less we will be inclined to make suggestions in the future.

'Not Invented Here' (NIH) syndrome

Another frequent reaction to ideas is a kind of automatic rejection, often for apparently 'excellent' reasons. But really we are opposing the proposal because it has not come from us and we subconsciously feel it somehow threatens us.

'Satisficing' and laziness

Sometimes, when we find what seems to be a solution to a problem, we choose not to look for any alternatives. This can be due to what has been called 'satisficing' (see Chapter 9, Negative Aspects of Groups). Satisficing can be due to simple laziness or else occur because we are so relieved to find an answer that we don't bother to look for a better one.

Mindset and assumptions

Many of us have a tendency to believe that our view of a situation is the one realistic view. So we don't make the effort of trying to put ourselves in someone else's position and imagining their point of view. If we were more prepared to question our own mindset and assumptions, we would more easily be able to think creatively about a range of possible solutions. Or else we can try to identify our basic assumptions – what we consider to be obvious – and question whether these have any real foundation. For example, some firms energetically struggled with the problem of how to make an electric car which could be easily recharged and wouldn't run the risk of being unusable when the batteries went flat. However, one company questioned why an electric car should only be electric. They then came up with a hybrid car which could run on electricity in towns (to minimize pollution) and on petrol in the country (recharging its own batteries in the process). Though this is not yet on the market, its development does show how quickly traditional assumptions about the nature of a product can be overturned.

38
Brainstorming

Background

Brainstorming was probably the first popularized technique for encouraging creative thinking in a group setting. The aim of a brainstorm is to generate the maximum number of ideas in a short period of time (usually half an hour to an hour). Brainstorming is not just a few people sitting around discussing an issue – such an approach would most likely only lead to analytical thinking and a review of old or existing ideas. For a brainstorm to generate truly creative and new ideas, certain conventions have to be followed.

There are three key features of a brainstorm which contribute to it being a forum for creative, rather than analytical thinking:

1. Generation of ideas is completely separated from evaluation. In a brainstorm the aim is to produce ideas, however ridiculous. At no time should any participant judge any idea or self-censor.
2. The purpose of gathering a group with different backgrounds is to expose people to other viewpoints and ideas, which they can pick up and build on. The group setting also encourages competition to produce the best ideas and humour, both of which are powerful forces in breaking down the barriers to creative thinking.
3. By setting quantity rather than quality of ideas as the goal, the session puts pressure on participants to try and go beyond limited, traditional ways of thinking.

Preparing a brainstorm

It is often difficult to move directly from the type of disciplined, analytical thinking required by normal work, to the way of thinking appropriate to a brainstorm. Some effective techniques for preparing a brainstorm are:

- Inform participants a couple of days in advance so they can give the matter some thought. If possible, visit each person, and explain the problem which will be discussed and how the session will be run
- At the start of the meeting present and agree with participants what the required behaviours will be – no evaluation of ideas; no self-censorship; build on other people's ideas; as many ideas as possible. These can be written on a sheet of paper and stuck on the wall, so they can be referred to during the meeting if people start to deviate from them.

• It can be helpful to begin by discussing the differences between analytical and creative thinking and how most people's creative side has been repressed by upbringing and education. This can release some frustration participants may have with always needing to be adult and logical. You should also mention some of the barriers to creative thinking as people can better overcome them if they are made aware of them.

Not all brainstorms lead to truly great ideas

The group chosen should all be able to contribute ideas to the solution of the problem, but should not be so closely involved and similar in position that they can only come up with a limited range of solutions. In organizations which have strong hierarchies or where departments are not used to working together, care must be taken when mixing people from different levels or functions. Otherwise you may have junior people playing up to what they think their superiors want to hear, or else some people being treated as outsiders by a central group. Both behaviours will constrain the creative generation of ideas.

Stating the problem

The brainstorm should begin with a statement of the problem and some background information, given either by the meeting chairman or the person who is most involved in the issue under discussion. Then a few minutes can be allowed for participants to ask questions to ensure they understand what is required. Often with problems which involve several departments, people can have quite different views about what the real problem is. For example, if discussing a general subject like how to improve profitability, each function will tend to see the solution lying in other functions' areas of responsibility. In this case, it may be necessary to have each person state what they believe the problem to be and then come to some agreement, which everyone can work with.

During the session

In the session, the chairman or meeting leader acts as a kind of traffic controller. Either he, or another person, should write all the ideas up, numbering each of them, with a felt pen on sheets of A1 paper. As each sheet is filled, it should be stuck on the wall, so that participants can see it throughout the session. In this way it can act as a stimulus to further ideas and be a visible record of what ideas have already been generated. The traffic controller ensures all ideas are recorded and that everyone gets a chance to speak. He should not go round the room asking people one by one for ideas, as this tends to inhibit creativity by putting pressure on participants to have ideas ready at specific times. Instead he should take ideas as they come, while trying to avoid one or two people dominating the meeting. The traffic controller is also responsible for making sure that the agreed behaviours are adhered to – that people do not evaluate ideas or criticize others' suggestions.

The meeting leader should try to encourage humour and wild thinking, but be careful not to direct people's thoughts too much in any one particular direction. When ideas begin to dry up, the meeting leader should make two or three attempts to start the flow again. This can be done by restating the problem in a different way, by asking if anyone wants to pick up and develop any recorded ideas, by suggesting participants imagine themselves in other roles and try to think how people in those roles would see the situation or by asking those present to think of an ideal, but totally unrealistic solution. All of these can set off completely new streams of thought. After this it is best to end the session, rather than trying to make it drag on when there clearly are no new ideas. While one can estimate the approximate duration of a session in advance, it should, if possible be allowed to run its natural course. What matters is not filling out the allotted time, but rather producing a number of new ideas.

After the session, participants will probably still be thinking about the problem and so may come up with some new and useful ideas. One way of capturing these is to have the ideas generated in the meeting typed up and a copy sent to all participants for them to review and add any new thoughts to.

Evaluating the ideas

There are many different ways of evaluating the ideas produced in a brainstorm. The whole group can be called together again, or just a smaller group of two or three people who are most closely involved in the problem, or the person who 'owns' the problem can perform the evaluation. Depending on the situation any of these may be appropriate. The key issue in deciding how to evaluate, is that there is no point brainstorming to produce new ideas if the evaluating group or person is only going to reject any which are either novel or else which do not fit in with his view of the situation. While evaluation is an analytical process, it must not be allowed to kill off all the new approaches which creative thinking has produced.

Ideas can be evaluated by classifying them into realistic and unrealistic, by rating them by ease of implementation, cost, likely results or whatever, by listing the advantages and disadvantages of each and so on. A judgement must be made as to which method is most suitable. Ideally, a short-list should be drawn up from which the final one or several ideas will be chosen.

Implementation

The aim of a brainstorm is to produce ideas, some of which will be implemented. Therefore it is important that there is, and that there is seen to be, some management action following a brainstorm, if possible involving some of the participants. If the session is followed by inertia or if further action is allowed to be drowned by operational problems or political opposition, then management will lose credibility, people will become cynical and the technique will be discredited. Brainstorming is a very visible activity and so must be followed by equally visible action.

39
Problem-solving

Problem-solving and brainstorming

A problem-solving meeting is a more recent development than brainstorming and there are some similarities between the two techniques. Both gather together a group of people to discuss a particular issue. Both require that participants free their minds to think creatively. However, while brainstorming restricts itself to creative thinking in order to generate the maximum number of ideas for later evaluation, problem-solving combines both creative and analytical thinking to generate ideas, evaluate them and then arrive at a decision which will be implemented.

Many management meetings, which have a certain problem-solving element, can appear confused and lacking in direction. Participants then become frustrated, so that emotional and political factors interfere with rational judgement, causing the results to be sub-optimum. One reason for this occurring is that people are working on different phases of the problem simultaneously – some may be thinking of solutions, others evaluating and others thinking how some proposal should be implemented. Because people's thinking is at different levels – some are in a creative mode, some analytical, some judgemental – communication starts to break down. A problem-solving meeting tries to avoid this, by distinguishing the different phases and taking all participants through each phase together.

Meeting structure

There are three main roles in a problem-solving meeting:

The client

The person who 'owns' the problem – that is to say, the person who is most affected by it and who wants to find a solution. He provides part of the 'content' – the problem to be discussed.

The meeting leader

Can also be called the enabler or the facilitator. He is responsible for the 'process' part of the meeting – for how the meeting runs, for helping clear communication and for traffic control so that ideas are heard and recorded. He guides the meeting through each phase and ensures that people behave in appropriate ways at each stage. Normally the leader will stick to the 'process' part of the meeting and make little or no contribution to the 'content'.

Resources

These are the other meeting participants, who will generate ideas, evaluate chosen solutions and contribute proposals for implementation. This is the other element of the meeting 'content'.

Different practitioners have different ways of running problem-solving meetings, but most include the following stages: problem statement, background to the problem, idea generation around solutions, choice of one or more solutions, identifying strengths and weaknesses of the chosen solutions, identification of what further actions are required, and finally decision on the next steps to be taken.

Running a problem-solving group

Choosing the group

A brainstorming group is just interested in idea generation. However, a problem-solving group has to arrive at and agree on a solution and the next steps. So it is necessary to have present those people who have the power to allow or veto the decision. The group chosen must have the authority to act on its own conclusions. If even one key decision-maker is missing, an important viewpoint may be lost and everything discussed will have to be reviewed with him later to get his approval.

Pre-presentation

As with a brainstorm, it is best to meet individually with all the participants a couple of days before the meeting to prepare them. This pre-presentation should be brief and should consist of informing them of the problem, the meeting procedure and what is expected of them.

Opening the meeting

This should start with a quick review of the agenda and an agreement on appropriate behaviours: only evaluate during the evaluation phase, don't criticize other people's ideas or try to defend your own, all ideas are good ideas, let other people finish talking before you propose an idea, try to give your ideas in short headlines rather than lengthy explanations, and so on. These guidelines should be written up on a sheet of A1 and stuck on the wall to be referred to if people start to deviate from what was agreed.

Stating the problem

The client should briefly state the problem, giving some background as to why it is a problem, what effects it has, what solutions have already been tried and any ideas he has for solving it. Then it may be useful to allow people a couple of minutes to question the client to ensure they have fully understood the issues. If there are widely different interpretations of the problem, it may be useful to have each member restate it in his own words and finally choose a formulation everyone feels they can work with.

Idea generation

This will be similar to a brainstorming. The principles are that as many ideas as possible should be generated, that participants should be stimulated by and build on each other's ideas, and that no evaluation or self-censorship should take place. Ideas should be written up on A1 by the meeting leader and stuck on the walls as in brainstorming.

Choice of solution

When ideas have been generated for ten to twenty minutes or when people are beginning to run dry, the meeting leader should ask the client to choose one or more to be analysed in more detail.

Strengths and weaknesses

The group should then take each of the chosen ideas in turn and identify their strengths and weaknesses. If participants start seeing only problems, they can be asked to first state what they like about an idea before going on to list what they believe to be weaknesses. This can often force them to open their minds to benefits which they had previously not noticed.

Final choice and next steps

Following the strengths and weaknesses analysis, the client makes a final choice of the one or several solutions, which will be implemented. He then agrees with the group what the next actions to be taken will be, who will be responsible for each, when they should be completed and whether the group should meet again to review progress.

Minutes and feedback

Within 24 hours of a problem-solving meeting, minutes of the meeting detailing the ideas, strengths and weaknesses analysis, final choice, next steps and responsibilities should be sent out to all participants. It can also be useful for the meeting leader to meet briefly again with each participant individually to get their reactions to the session. If enthusiasm or a dominant character caused the meeting to go off course, this is the time when this can be picked up and action taken.

Criticisms and strengths

The problem-solving approach has been criticized on two main counts. It has been suggested that people cannot easily move from rational thinking before the meeting, to creative thinking in the idea generation stage, back to analytical thinking in the evaluation phase. Also, when the client makes his short-list of solutions or final choice of solution, this can come as a kind of anti-climax after all the energy of the creative-thinking phase. Moreover, participants who feel the client has ignored their solutions or simply made the wrong choice can quickly become frustrated and withdraw or become disruptive.

However, by providing a structure, where everybody moves through the problem-solving process together, this approach can cut out much of the mis-communication, disjointedness, lack of clarity and disagreement which less structured problem-solving can produce. Moreover, the clear structure and emphasis on one person being responsible for the important 'process' part of the session can significantly reduce the emotional and political factors which often prevent problem-solving from being rational.

40
Mind-mapping

Background

The technique of mind-mapping was originated by the psychologist, broadcaster and writer, Tony Buzan.[12] Mind maps are apparently straightforward, yet extremely versatile tools. They can be used by individuals or in a group setting. They can act as a way of liberating the mind from the constraints of logical, analytical thinking. They can also serve as a method for learning and remembering, which can be many times more powerful than note-taking and memorizing.

Linear and associative thinking

When we communicate we usually use whole, logical sentences. This tendency to express ourselves in a linear fashion is reinforced by the linearity of the printed word. If we were asked to spend a few minutes preparing a talk on any subject, most of us would start to write down a list of ideas, possibly with a few headlines and some detail under each headline. Yet the mind works in an 'associative' rather than linear way. Each idea or thought we have does not necessarily lead logically to the next, but can spark off a whole series of associations, which may be based on logic, sound, smell, colour, memories, feel or whatever.

In spoken and written communication each thought is like a step in a certain direction, but in our mind it is a nucleus which, if allowed, can shoot out bridges in many different directions. Thus there is constant tension between the limited way we are forced to communicate and the expansive way the mind works. Faced with this conflict, most of us learn to discipline our thoughts to fit in with our communication patterns and so lose much of the richness of what is going on in our minds. By trying to replicate the 'associative' nature of our thought processes, mind-mapping seeks to capture some of this richness, which is normally lost.

Constructing a mind map

The figure is a simple example of a mind map done in less than two minutes on 'the role of management'.

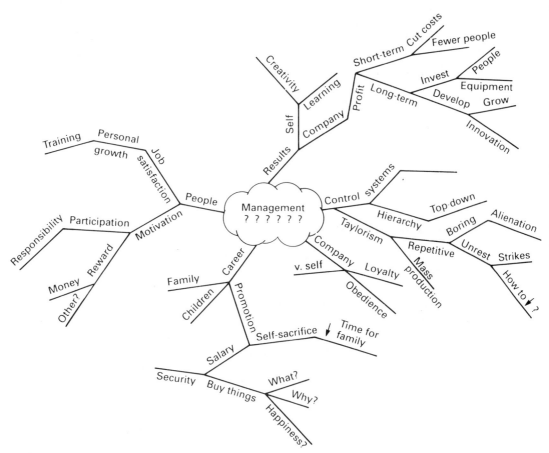

Figure 12

As can be seen, even a very quick mind map can generate a wide range of ideas and trains of thought compared to a standard listing of ideas. If, for example, you were preparing a talk, a two- or three-minute mind-map could give enough material for up to an hour or more. Or if you are looking for a solution to a particular problem, a mind map can rapidly give you a huge number of different leads to follow. (At the end of this chapter is the central part of a mind map used to write the chapter on trade unions as an example of how the mind map can open up new directions.)

Steps in mind-mapping

The mind map works by allowing any idea to spark off other ideas. So as any thought occurs, it is recorded on the mind map even if, at the time, it is not logically connected to any other thought. Each branch of a mind map will generally contain related thoughts, but you can jump around from one branch to another as ideas arise.

The first step is to put the subject in the centre. This can be a word, a drawing, a symbol or whatever. Then as thoughts occur to you, you start to build branches out from the central issue. The branches should sprout out from each other to reflect the way each thought leads to another. If you should have a completely new train of thought, you should start a new series of branches. Any thoughts should be captured in one or at most two words, otherwise the whole structure becomes cluttered and difficult to follow.

Once you have finished drawing all the branches you can think of, you can draw circles round each major area of ideas and then begin to order your thoughts. It is at this point that you start to apply analytical procedures to choose what is relevant and what can be discarded. Mind-mapping is a rapid and powerful way of generating a large variety of thoughts; analysis and action should then follow.

Mind maps and memory

At least 70 per cent (and probably more) of the words we hear or read are irrelevant to the basic subject-matter. They are mostly introduction, detail, description and so on. In textbooks, especially business books, there are often just a few basic facts and a vast amount of build-up, filling, examples, repetition and general meandering. The normal way we have of reading, taking notes and remembering is through whole sentences and phrases presented in a linear fashion. Thus we fill our minds with a great amount of irrelevant material. By mind-mapping the contents of a book, lecture, speech or meeting, we only pick out the key words and associations and present them in a visual fashion. Then when trying to recall, or re-present, what we have learnt – if we decide to produce a mind map – the key words and associations will automatically generate a huge amount of detail which we could never have remembered, if we had tried to memorize it. Mind-mapping can thus turn remembering from being hard work into a creative, associative process.

Mind-mapping in groups

As well as being a powerful way for an individual to liberate himself from unilinear thought processes, a mind map can be extremely effective in helping a group break new ground or get a new insight into an old problem. Any group which spends five or ten minutes doing a quick mind map round an issue can normally generate many more times the number of ideas that an analytical approach can – though once the idea generation is over, of course, analytical and judgemental processes need to be applied to the result. Like brainstorming and the creative part of problem-solving the key point to remember is that, for a period, ideas should be allowed to flow freely without any evaluation, criticism or comments like 'we've tried that before'.

Moreover, like the other creative thinking techniques, by dividing a group's discussion clearly into creative and analytical phases, mind maps can help avoid some of the confusion and mingling of emotional and political with rational feelings, which often is a part of normal problem resolution.

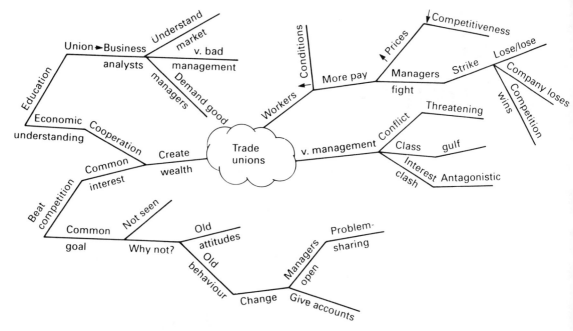

Figure 13 Example of the central part of a mind map looking at how to improve the part played by trade unions

41
Quality circles

There are many myths surrounding quality circles – for example, some experts have attributed most of Japan's extraordinary success in raising quality to quality circles alone. While they have no doubt made a significant contribution, the role they can play, though important, is limited. Another great myth is that quality circles are something totally new. The basis for quality circles already exists and

Sometimes people lower down in the organization can have the best ideas

has always existed. Every time two or more employees gather and bemoan some management decision or other, the bad performance of an inappropriate machine the engineers thought was suitable, the material they have to work with, the conditions they work under, the inadequate instructions they are given, all these could be seen as spontaneous, informal quality circles. What is new, is that management have woken up to the fact that those who do the work might have fresh insights to contribute. So management are adopting quality circles as a way of formally harnessing workers' knowledge and ideas to improve organizations' performance.

If introduced correctly and in the right environment, quality circles can be extremely effective. But if insufficient thought is given to why, when and how they are started, they can end up giving a few quick results and then leading to disruption, conflict and demotivation.

History

In the 1950s Japanese goods deservedly had the reputation for appalling quality. Yet by the 1970s they were looked up to in most fields as being the best quality available. Quality circles were just one of several techniques used to achieve this incredible transformation.

One source claims that quality circles first appeared in the US in the 1950s. But most other references locate their origin in Japan in 1962 or early 1963. They quickly spread to major Japanese firms and it has been estimated that by the early 1980s, there were around one million circles involving about ten million employees. In the 1980s, as Western companies tried to discover the secret of Japan's success, quality circles were seized on as providing one of the answers. This may have been due more to the fact that they are easy to understand and implement, than to the real role they actually played. Western management have had a tendency to look for simple fashionable solutions, in preference to dealing with more difficult basic problems.

Structure

A quality circle normally consists of a small group of workers meeting on a regular basis with their foreman or supervisor to discuss, analyse and try to solve any issues concerned with quality, productivity, work conditions or planning and control systems. The theoretical basis is that an organization should try to continuously raise its performance through making small, incremental improvements and that, in many cases, because they are closest to operating problems, workers will be able to develop possible solutions. Also, by involving workers in decision-making about their work environment, quality circles can increase their sense of responsibility, their dignity and their motivation.

In setting up quality circles some training is usually given to workers and supervisors in methods of investigation and analysis of operating systems, for example, statistical process control, or Ishikawa (fishbone) cause-and-effect diagrams. Additionally there is normally some time dedicated to improving participants' communication and meeting skills.

Results

The typical results recorded are:

- Increases in productivity, safety, delivery performance, morale and communications;

- A greater awareness of how different functions are inter-related and a reduction of departments being isolated from one another;
- Responsibility for quality can be shifted from the inspection department to operators;
- Greater commitment from workers, less absenteeism and conflict;
- Improved work environment, making it easier to introduce change.

Implementing quality circles

Some key features of the Japanese environment into which quality circles were introduced are that many companies were already well on the way to improving quality before starting quality circles, most companies had highly committed work-forces and most companies also had major programmes of investment in automation and modernization. A similar situation often does not exist in Western firms.

Quality circles pose two basic questions to the organization:

1. What percentage of operating improvements can actually be addressed by the workers, compared to those which are the responsibility of management, engineering, purchasing, marketing, personnel and so on?
2. Is management really prepared to accept the shift of power down to workers, which quality circles always require?

If most of the operating or quality problems come from outside the workers' control, then the quality circle will quickly bring to management's attention the need for certain actions to be taken by other functions. If these actions are not taken, the members of the circle will tend to become disillusioned and the quality circle will fail.

As they give some responsibility for decision-making to workers' groups, quality circles must be accompanied by a genuine desire to encourage participation and to devolve power down through the organization. If they are part of 'lifeboat democracy' – management are trying them, because everything else has failed – workers will know this, and see them as attempts by management to have the workers sort out management's problems, while management get the credit and the pay. Or if, when the circle starts to suggest changes in systems or improvements in equipment, management start to act defensively, again workers will quickly become aware of the limits of their field of influence and disillusionment will tend to follow.

For quality circles to be successful most of the following should apply:

- There should already be some commitment from the work-force and some genuine trust between management and employees.
- There should be some real operating problems the circle can deal with. Quality circles should not be used just as indirect ways of trying to increase productivity.
- Management should be prepared to accept the consequences of eliciting employees' opinions – that management and the firm may come under heavy criticism.
- Management must have the power to, and be willing to, act on reasonable proposals made by the circles.

- Setting the circles up must include training for workers in problem-solving, creative thinking, running meetings, communication and presentations.
- If the quality circle is to run alongside or replace a suggestions scheme which gave financial rewards, then the circle may have to be given some incentive. Otherwise it will be perceived as the organization trying to get suggestions without having to pay for them.
- The circle should not be viewed by workers as the latest fashionable idea to be picked up, imposed on the company and quickly forgotten by a management, which tends to latch on to every 'new' trend. Nor should it be the last desperate attempt to improve performance made by a management bankrupt of ideas.

The general experience of quality circles in the West is that initially they are successful, as a few obvious operating problems, lived with for years, are finally dealt with. But then as the circle starts to consider more fundamental issues, it finds that the new 'democracy' has very clear limits and disaffection and apathy quickly set in.

If the organization is hierarchical, controlled from the top and has a history of excluding employees from participation in decision-making, quality circles are unlikely to work in the long term. The implementation of quality circles has to be accompanied by a genuine attempt to spread power through an organization and to invest in developing employees, rather than just seeing them as a cost to be controlled. After years of reducing its personnel through automation and through replacing skilled full-time workers with unskilled part-time staff, one company decided to introduce quality circles. Quite clearly, there was little trust between management and employees. Moreover, most of those who could have made a genuine contribution had been replaced by 'cheaper' part-timers. The experiment was a failure.

Although quality circles appear simple and easy to implement, for them to be successful they often need a little more thought and effort than some companies are willing to give. But a successful quality circle implementation can be the basis for major operational improvements. Experience has shown that quality circles are most effective when a firm is already some way along the road to making quality improvements – quality circles are often best at squeezing out the last results, when the basic work has already been started. When quality circles have been established at the very start of a quality programme or are viewed as the firm's quality salvation, they have normally been disappointments. They are a useful tool if used correctly, but like other problem-solving techniques, they are only a small part of the improvement process – they need to lead to positive action by management.

42
Other creative thinking techniques

The techniques discussed below are designed to be used in conjunction with brainstorming, problem-solving, mind-mapping and quality circles, to help break through the barriers preventing us finding new, creative solutions to problems.

The 'ridiculous idea' or the 'perfect world' scenario

Studies of great breakthroughs have repeatedly shown that they are often not made by careful logical incremental steps forward. The tendency is for a sudden, illogical flash of inspiration to occur and then for the person to work backwards from the breakthrough to see logically whether it can be justified.

When faced with a problem, it is frequently better to try and emulate the 'breakthrough' process, than to work analytically towards a solution. This has been called both the 'ridiculous idea' method and the 'perfect world' scenario – the first, because you should think of an answer which is quite ridiculous in practical terms, yet does solve the problem, and the second, because you imagine the solution which you would apply in a 'perfect world'.

Once you have your ridiculous, ideal solution you should list its strengths and weaknesses – why it is a good solution and why it is unrealistic. Then you should work backwards from the solution, gradually modifying it to make it more and more practical, while keeping as many of the strengths as possible. Normally you will soon reach an implementable solution, which is much better than any you could have built up logically.

A brief example might be: A company is faced by a claim for higher pay and/or a shorter working week. The standard solution might be to prepare for negotiation in the hope of trading off a part of what is demanded for an improvement in productivity. The ridiculous solution could be expressed as 'if the workers had to run this company, they'd soon realise how tough the competitive environment is'. Of course, you're not going to hand the firm over to the employees. But the ridiculous idea does suggest a line of thought – how to make the workers more aware of the difficulty of being competitive? This in its turn suggests a whole stream of possible actions: support union representatives (time off and money) to go on part-time business courses, arrange in-house courses for the unions or key workers, have union representation on the board, develop participative decision-making, implement quality circles, offer staff more on-the-job training, start giving shares as part of a profit-sharing scheme and so on. The ridiculous idea has thus led to a long-term programme of actions to improve employee commitment, bridge the gulf between management and staff, and reduce conflict.

Return to obstacles

When faced with a seemingly intractable problem, many of us work away at the issue, often with diminishing effectiveness. This is particularly true in group situations, where the more a problem is worked on, the more frustration, emotions and interpersonal factors will interfere with a rational solution. And as the group becomes tired and cooperation becomes less productive, the less the group will be able to work effectively on any other issues. Most of us are familiar with meetings where the first or second item on the agenda took most of the time, leaving insufficient time and energy for effective discussion of the other issues.

An obvious way to avoid this is to move on to other issues and return later to any major obstacles. This has several consequences. When going beyond an obstacle, it will often appear different from the other side, making the solution much easier. Moreover, when solving other issues you may get extra information or insights, which render the initial obstacle less formidable. In addition, problem-solving is dependent on the momentum and motivation of the problem-solver. If you remain floundering at a certain point, your energy will be dissipated; if you deal with other issues and gain some momentum, you will more easily be able to cope with the obstacle. This is especially important with groups, where much of the group's effectiveness comes not from individuals, but from group dynamics. So the key with groups is to have the group successfully deal with easier issues, to create the dynamics and then to pitch the functioning group at the main obstacle. The common mistake with groups is to begin a meeting with a difficult problem, as this can prevent the group ever reaching an effective mode of operation.

Relying on the subconscious

Although we may decide to take a break from dealing with a particular problem, our mind usually continues to work on the issue. And given time it often comes up with a solution. For some people this happens while taking exercise; for others while sleeping; for some it's when they wake up; for others it can be while eating or taking a bath. But the result is the same: the mind seems to carry on independently and to open new doors which we were unable to find. It is thus often more constructive to admit you won't get any further and to allow your subconscious to mull an issue over for a while, rather than forcing yourself to find a solution which just will not come. Learning to take a break and relax can often be a more effective method of problem-solving than excessive hard work.

Positive phrasing

By thinking or speaking in a positive manner, we can frequently encourage ourselves and others to find new and positive ideas. Our everyday speech is full of almost automatic responses like 'yes, but . . .' and 'I agree, but the problem is . . .' and 'the difficulty is . . .'. In fact these sound much more natural to us than if someone said, 'yes, and what's more . . .' or 'I like your idea and suggest . . .'. These latter, positive phrases sound stilted and artificial, whereas the former, negative ones appear more authentic. Yet, because they are negative they close doors, kill ideas, look for obstacles and demotivate those who hear them.

If we can bring ourselves to express our problems in terms like 'I wish we could . . .' or 'how can we . . .', we will motivate others to try and help us, rather than having them agree with the difficulty of our predicament. If we can always make it a discipline of first saying what we like about someone's idea, before expressing concerns, we will stimulate them to think of solutions. By starting with concerns, we give a negative response, which will only discourage and lead to withdrawal. While this positive approach may appear 'forced' and unnatural, we may find it interesting to reflect on how it is that negative responses have become a natural part of our communication, whereas positive ones somehow jar with what we consider normal.

Headlining

When presenting an idea to a group, there are two general approaches we can take. Either we can build up to our conclusion by taking the group through our evidence and thought processes, or else we can give our conclusion first in a brief headline and then go into any explanation later. The first approach is that which is favoured by classical logic – you build up an irrefutable case, piece by piece, so that the final conclusion becomes inevitable. However, with the classical model, while others listen to us, they will have to use most of their creative energy trying to follow us and working out where we are heading. With the second approach, people immediately learn our goal and while listening to our explanation can start thinking about building on our ideas.

The classical, logical build-up model is obviously essential when making major presentations or presenting a new strategy and so on. But in less formal, group problem-solving arenas the headline-first approach may be a much more effective use of other people's time and creative energies.

LESSONS FROM JAPAN

43 Japan and the West

44 'Market share' versus 'financial' strategy

45 Maximize customer satisfaction

46 The importance of quality

47 Just-in-time production

48 Getting the best from people

49 Role of the trade unions

43
Japan and the West

There is a huge mythology surrounding Japan's commercial success over the last twenty to thirty years and there have been many ingenious interpretations and misinterpretations of Japan's rise in prosperity. Some people believe that the Japanese have some unique cultural characteristic, which has helped them out-compete the West. Other experts have suggested that Japan is only the latest in a long line of models for managers to learn from – in the 1950s it was the USA, in the early 1960s Germany, in the late 1960s Sweden, in the 1970s and 1980s Japan and in the 1990s it may be Korea.

One reason which has been cited as important in Japan's economic progress is its geography and population. Japan consists of small, mountainous islands with only around 10 per cent of the land arable. It has few natural resources and over one hundred million people to feed. The only way such a country can survive is through importing raw materials, processing them to add value and then exporting them. The argument goes that lacking the large internal market found in the USA or Europe, the Japanese have been driven to become export-oriented. Yet there are other countries which share the same physical features which have been nowhere near as successful.

But the key issue, when examining the Japanese experience, is not necessarily to try and fully understand what is behind it, in order to find some formula which will magically guarantee a Western organization's success. Rather, what is important is to compare Japanese practices with those in the West, to see what insights can be gained into why so many Western companies are failing to be competitive, as these insights may provide useful guides as to what improvements should be made. A first step in this process is to identify the major cultural differences between Japan and the West.

Differences in attitude between Japan and the West

While it would be difficult to do a complete cultural comparison, the table opposite does try to single out some key characteristics where Japan and the West appear to diverge.[13]

JAPAN	THE WEST
Sense of racial uniqueness	Individual uniqueness
Many ways of seeing an issue	One right answer
Acceptance of status quo	Independence/confidence in self to effect change
Self-effacement	Aggressiveness
Responsibility to and for the group	Narrow responsibilities (to oneself)
Respect for learning	Doubtful of learning
Harmony in everything	Love of debate/confrontation
Faith in work	Dislike of work
Job rotation in one organization	Functional specialization working for several organizations
National interest	Self-interest

Driving force – family
        – company
        – group/society
	Driving force – self
	        – money
	        – personal status

Most profits go back into the company	Most profits go to shareholders

Objectives of Japanese management

A number of studies have been carried out comparing the priorities of Japanese and Western top management. One commentator proposed the following priorities:

USA
1. Return on investment
2. Share price increase

Japan
1. Increase market share
2. Return on investment

A study in the UK showed that 93 per cent of a group of British directors felt that 'short-term profits' were their company's main objective, compared with 40 per cent of a comparable group of Japanese directors.[14] Looking at the comparative work which has been done, a number of factors emerge as possibly significantly more important to Japanese managers, than to their counterparts in the West:

- long-term viewpoint;
- total organizational integration – crossing barriers between disciplines;
- customer-orientation;
- constant incremental improvement – often using workers' ideas;
- sales-led – market share goals;
- high level of employee training;

- sub-contract to maintain flexibility;
- cooperative relations with suppliers;
- flexibility and adaptability;
- group and company success.

Four key differences

There appear to be four main differences between the Japanese and Western business environments which may partially account for the marked difference in economic performance:

1. Role of the government

Unlike many Western governments, the Japanese government has had the consistent long-term objective of helping the whole country be successful economically. It has achieved this not through nationalization nor through pumping millions into industries which were clearly no longer competitive. In fact, it has allowed many non-competitive industries to disappear. What the Japanese government has done is to promote the idea that international trade is the only way the country can survive and as part of this to give economic and legal encouragement to what it perceived as being the key industries of the future. In the 1950s the government pushed companies to invest in steel-making because it saw steel as being crucial to the country's economic growth. At the start of the 1990s, it designated the following as 'priority industries': bio-technology, genetic engineering, aerospace, fifth generation computers, information technology. And it identified a number of 'encouraged technologies': fine ceramics, separation diaphragms, crystalline macro-molecules and conductive macromolecules. Over at least thirty years, the Japanese government has pushed firms to invest in what were seen as industries of the future, rather than fighting to prop up industries of the past.

2. Long-term approach to strategy

The concept the Japanese have of business strategy seems to be different from that of many Western firms on several counts.

Western strategy is strongly aimed at increasing shareholder wealth, while Japanese strategy is directed at growing and strengthening the corporation. Moreover, because Western companies are concerned with maintaining share price to protect themselves against hostile take-overs, they are pushed into trying to maximize profit in the short term, even if this damages their longer-term prospects. As hostile take-overs are virtually unknown in Japan and as financial institutions are more interested in long-term growth, firms can have a much longer strategic perspective.

Linked to this is a difference in view about how profits are produced. With their long-term outlook, Japanese firms see investment driving growth, which will lead to profits. But because of the pressures to show short-term results to bolster up share price, many Western firms do not have the time to rely on growth and so are forced to shore up profitability through tight financial control, rationalization and cutbacks.

3. Concept of the corporation

In Japanese corporations there is a much greater focus on the human element than in Western firms. In the West, firms are mainly driven by financial imperatives and members, especially managers, view their jobs as temporary stages in a career which will normally include several employers – loyalty is to oneself, not the company. Many Japanese corporations, particularly the largest ones, have succeeded in having their members identify their welfare with the well-being of the firm. Their corporate missions are expressed in terms of a challenge to their members, rather than in terms of maximizing shareholder wealth. Moreover, as their employees expect to spend much of their lives in one or two firms, they realize they will inherit the consequences of their own decisions and so are inclined to work towards the general good and not look for quick, career-enhancing results.

4. The creation of wealth

In the West, where share prices can rise or plummet based more on shareholder gambling than on the real performance of firms, the acts of earning money and creating wealth have become disassociated. Huge amounts of money can be earned through management buy-outs, junk bonds, acquisition, corporate raiding and so on. Yet none of these activities actually creates wealth for companies or countries. If anything, they only cause disruption and saddle corporations with heavy levels of debt, which drain away much of their resources. In Japan firms are not victims of the whims of financial markets nor of the ingenious schemes of financial wizards. Japanese companies do not grow through buying, dismembering and selling off other companies. If they wish to grow, it must be through internal growth. Wealth is thus not seen as something which can be magically produced through wheeling and dealing or through creative accounting – it is clearly linked to investment and growth.

44
'Market share' versus 'financial' strategy

The diagram below gives a number of different ways a firm can approach the issue of improving long-term profitability.

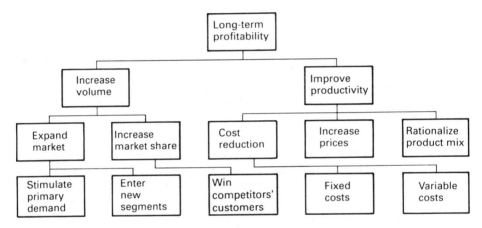

Figure 14

Western strategy

As stated in the previous section, many Western companies are under considerable pressure to maintain a high share price and high level of dividends to shareholders. These pressures exist for several reasons. As shareholders are often interested in maximizing their wealth in the short term, they will stay clear of companies which do not show a commitment to supporting share price and dividends. Poor performance in the short term will also be picked up by the financial press and seen as a comment on the abilities of top management. In addition, any decline in share price makes a company vulnerable to take-over.

So companies who are forced to report their results quarterly or half-yearly will tend to work within these time-frames. Major development projects, basic research and consistent policy are all aspects which will usually be neglected where the focus is on the short-term bottom line. The reaction of several European and American firms to Japanese competitive pressures was to cut investments, reduce staff, reduce R & D and abandon new product development

– to work on the elements contained on the right-hand side of the diagram. The immediate result was, naturally, improved profitability, which was often reflected in a strong share price. However, in the medium term, by reducing their manufacturing base and not defending their market shares, such firms fell into the vicious circle of less volume leading to higher unit costs, leading to lower margins, leading to more cuts and so on.

A very typical scenario is for a Japanese firm to attack a market by moving into the lowest price segment. Western companies withdraw from the segment, justifying their actions by claiming the Japanese have the advantage of lower labour costs, and anyway they are only interested in retaining the high value added and high margin segments. Having captured the high volume low price segment, the Japanese move up into the next segment, the Western firms withdraw again, once again with plausible reasons. But each time a Western firm retreats, it loses volume, its costs per unit rise and it becomes less competitive. Finally it will run out of market segments to retreat to and good reasons for not trying to compete with the Japanese.

The accountancy gap

Another reason Western firms seem to focus on the right-hand side of the diagram rather than the left (on profit through financial control rather than market share growth) may be the predominance of people with a financial background. A study in Britain showed that while around 90 per cent of firms sampled had a financial director on the main board, only about 50 per cent had a marketing director.[15] While an international comparison made in 1986/87 showed considerably more qualified accountants in countries like America, Britain and France, than there were in the most successful economies, such as West Germany and Japan:[16]

Country	Number of Qualified Accountants
Japan	6,000
West Germany	4,000
USA	300,000
Britain	120,000
France	20,000

This apparent imbalance in numbers of accountants will affect companies in two main ways. Most obviously, people with backgrounds in finance will tend to look for financial solutions to company problems. This generally results in an emphasis on control rather than growth. But there is also the problem that in many countries standard accounting procedures are based on systems developed at the start of this century and these have largely failed to keep up with modern methods of measuring performance. This has created a gap between what accounts measure and what is happening in reality. For example, normal methods for examining the viability of any investment are based on calculating the payback period (usually using a discounted cash flow or net present value method). But such an approach fails to take into account the results of increased flexibility and ability to meet customer delivery schedules, improvements in quality, shorter product launch times, long-term R & D and improvements in performance through higher morale and better utilization of employee skills.

Another problem arises because many firms' costing systems allocate overhead costs according to direct labour costs. This was fine when direct labour was the major part of product cost. But now that direct labour is often less than 10 per cent of total costs, such a method can give a very misleading picture. This can cause firms to have misguided notions of which products have the highest margins and is likely to lead to wrong pricing and marketing decisions.

After ten to fifteen years of rationalization, cost control, slimming down, product range consolidation and productivity improvements, many Western firms have succeeded in improving profitability. However, they now find themselves with a reduced manufacturing base competing in markets dominated by Japanese companies. Moreover, many of their suppliers have disappeared and so they are dependent in some areas (microchips, machine tools, industrial robots) on Japanese companies for many of their parts.

Market share strategy

Most Japanese firms have adopted an approach which is based on the left-hand side of the diagram – achieving profitability through expansion of markets and increasing market share. This has allowed them quickly and profitably to dominate markets which were thought to be mature or declining, and often to grow these markets. As was shown in the section on strategy, the types of strategic model used by Western firms, such as portfolio analysis, tend to lead to defeatist, defensive policies which almost encourage firms to give up in markets which they believe to be saturated. But as Yamaha have shown with pianos and Honda with motorcycles, the idea that a market is mature is only the mental state of someone who is unable to think of an innovatory way of reinjecting energy into the market.

The cost benefits of being a market leader are obvious. There are economies of scale to be gained throughout the supply chain. By buying larger volumes, you can purchase materials cheaper. There are lower unit costs in manufacturing, goods handling, administration, distribution and selling. Also, advertising costs can be spread over a greater volume, allowing the brand leader to have a larger budget than competitors, while still maintaining the most favourable cost structure.

These economies are then exaggerated by the distribution and display system. Because of pressure on space, retailers will tend to display only two to three brands. Often one of these is the retailer's own brand. The brand leader will normally be in a strong position in relation to negotiating with the retailer, as the retailer probably has to stock the brand leader's products. But the firms which are number two, three or four in the market have a much tougher fight to obtain distribution space. Too frequently, this is only achieved at the cost of substantial price discounts to retailers. A study in Britain of a number of consumer goods markets indicated how great a difference there could be between the profitability of the market leader and other competitors:

Position in Market	Net Margin (%)
1	17.9
2	2.8
3	−0.9
4	−5.9

Japanese companies have even been known to lose money in certain markets for as much as five or ten years. But they are willing to do this, as they know that eventually when they finally exhaust their Western competitors and emerge as market leader, high profitability is virtually guaranteed. For example, Honda made losses in several European motorcycle markets for several years before becoming a highly profitable market leader. Few Western companies could take such an approach. The financial markets and managers' careers would not allow it.

When Japanese companies do start to dominate their markets, they tend to use their strong financial position to generate cash for research and development and advertising. They then defend their positions through constant product improvements, frequent new models and heavy advertising expenditure. It is hard to see how Western companies, tied to satisfying the short-termism of the financial markets, can compete with this strategy of aggressive market share growth.

45
Maximize customer satisfaction

One commentator highlighted a fundamental difference between the business philosophies of some Western and some Japanese companies, when he talked of Western firms trying to de-skill their workers and de-skill their customers.[17] Workers were de-skilled by having their jobs split into simple repetitive tasks, through having automation imposed on them and through their performance being monitored by tightly-structured management control systems. Customers were de-skilled by a never-ending stream of poor-quality products, through patronizing advertising, through heavy-handed selling pressure and through constantly being told that minor changes to existing products were 'totally new', 'exciting' and 'different'.

Against this he proposed that Japanese companies had tried to create a highly-educated skilled work-force and had tried to develop products which were aimed at selling because of consumers' desire for them, rather than due to massive advertising and sales support. His suggestion was that the driving force of many Western companies was to sell what they could produce, whereas Japanese competitors had moved in the direction of trying to make what the consumers wanted. He believed that Western firms still had a production or sales orientation, while Japanese companies had developed a marketing orientation.

Putting the customer first

It has become fashionable in the West to talk of 'putting the customer first'. One portrayal of this is replacing the traditional organizational pyramid with the boss at the top, by one where the customer is at the top. Another is to see the various functions of the organization as being in a circle around the customer, who is central. Michael Porter's idea of a company's suppliers, internal activities, and distributors all being part of a 'value chain' whose aim is creating 'value' for the customer provides further expression of this idea of organizations being driven by their customers, rather than customers being cajoled into accepting what organizations can offer.[18]

Most firms probably believe they do put the customer first. After all it is common sense that unless you satisfy your customers you cannot survive. But, in reality, many firms are still driven by the requirements of production, engineering, finance or sales so that their products gradually fall out of line with what their customers want. The oil companies have not put their customers first with the way they appeared to delay the introduction of lead-free petrol and have given the impression of operating price-fixing agreements. Airlines, though claiming to be customer-oriented, spend a considerable amount of time and resources protecting their monopoly on the most profitable routes in order to charge excessive prices. And the fact that nine out of ten new grocery products flop suggests that they were initially created more to satisfy the needs of the marketing department and advertising agency, than to meet any real, identified customer need.

A policy of putting the customer first has some important implications:

- Strategies like cost-cutting, product range rationalization, consolidation and so on cannot be a result of satisfying customer needs.
- They can only be due to a failure to match customers' needs. So though they may be necessary in the short term to ensure a firm's survival, unless they are accompanied by clear plans to better serve customers, they can never in themselves be a serious contribution to the firm's long-term success.
- Firms must continually ask the questions 'what needs do my products satisfy?' and 'are there any better ways of satisfying those needs?' This is to say they must focus on why the customer buys the product rather than the details of the product they sell. Otherwise they may end up continuously adding refinements to products which consumers no longer want.
- If your aim is to be the cheapest then you are probably not really producing something which satisfies customers better than competitive products. Therefore you are forced into trying to boost sales through low price. This may be successful in the short term, but it is unlikely to give you very attractive margins. Moreover, your constant focus on keeping costs and prices down is probably distracting your attention from the issue of identifying what your customers actually want. So if price is becoming your main competitive weapon, you may find you are only buying time and not actively improving your competitive position.

Role of market research

Much of the market research done in the West is commissioned through advertising agencies and is directed at measuring the effectiveness of massive advertising campaigns, rather than consumers' actual satisfaction with products. As advertising agencies are normally paid a percentage of their clients' advertising spend, it is in their interest to boost clients' spending – for example, by convincing their clients of the necessity of maintaining higher consumer awareness than competitors. Market researchers, who often depend on advertising agencies for their livelihood, can be reluctant to judge any advertising campaign too harshly and this can sometimes influence the way they present their results.

All this can lead to firms being so taken up with their advertising efforts that they start to overlook the need to constantly monitor how consumers actually feel about their products and whether these products are still satisfying consumer needs. When the Japanese attacked the American car market in the 1970s, there was no way they could match the advertising spend of Ford,

General Motors and Chrysler. But because they had identified consumer needs and supplied the right products – smaller, more efficient, higher quality cars – they were able to succeed in spite of the Americans' heavy advertising. Of course, there is a need to advertise and obviously advertising effectiveness must be measured, but many companies have confused this activity with real marketing and are not paying enough attention to the basic function of marketing – identifying and satisfying consumer needs.

A broader view of the customer

Some Japanese companies have tried to broaden the idea of the customer by encouraging their workers to treat other workers in the factory as customers. This approach can help heighten workers' awareness of what type of quality and service is needed by the work stations subsequent to their operation. Moreover, it can lead to departments like engineering, design, purchasing and so on focusing more on their part in providing a service to other functions, rather than becoming too involved in their particular discipline to the detriment of the rest of the organization.

There are a number of Western companies where there is a need to encourage departments to become more conscious of how their work affects other departments. From this base they can move to a position of starting to view other functions as their customers and develop action plans to improve the quality of the products and services they supply to other areas.

46
The importance of quality

Over the last thirty years the Japanese have gone from being the makers of cheap, second-rate, shoddy goods to being seen as the leaders in quality products in a huge number of markets. While Western companies could once charge higher prices for their superior quality, they are now commonly viewed as the cheap alternative to better Japanese goods. Moreover, by offering high quality, Japanese companies have increased consumers' expectations of the quality of the products they buy. This has put Western firms, who have been unable to improve their quality to the same extent, in a weak competitive position, often leaving them price cuts as the only way of fighting back.

That the West should now be learning about quality from Japanese companies is ironic. Four of the main exponents of the importance of quality were American (see below) and their theories were mostly developed in the 1940s and 1950s. However, at that time Western firms were mainly interested in satisfying consumer demand, which outstripped supply. So there was no real need to pay too much attention to significantly improving quality. The Japanese, however, saw quality as a way of quickly becoming competitive and adopted much of the teaching of people like W. Edwards Deming, Joseph M. Juran, Armand V. Feigenbaum and Philip B. Crosby. Deming and Juran spent considerable time in Japan in the 1950s and 1960s, while many American companies were not interested in their work. There is even a Deming Quality medal awarded annually in Japan, although many businessmen in the West have never heard of him.

Difference in concept of quality

Even today, there appears to be a fundamental difference between the way that Japanese and Western firms view quality. For example, a recent Western textbook said that with 'enough expenditure' almost anything could be given high quality and reliability.[19] For managers in the West, achieving high quality is often seen as expensive. So they usually try to establish an acceptable level of quality at the right price. Many of the ways Western managers use statistical quality control, inspection and setting targets of a certain number of defects per thousand parts are static rather than pro-active – they believe that there will always be a certain level of defects and try to control this within what they have decided is an 'acceptable' range. So theoretically, with this approach, any complex product (like a car) with several thousand parts will tend to contain a few which are defective.

By adopting such theories as Total Quality Control and Zero Defects, Japanese companies have taken a much more pro-active approach. Rather than aiming at so many defects per thousand, they have targets of defects per million parts. This creates an environment where the organization is continuously trying to improve quality performance. The table gives some examples of what this difference in concept means in practice.

	The West	*Japan*
Concept of quality	Static	Continuous improvement
Focus of activity	Volume/profit	Quality/customer satisfaction
Quality responsibility	QC department	Mainly workers
Quality training	For QC staff	For all workers
Solving quality problems	Probably QC staff and engineering	Employees, supervisors and management
Quality targets	Set by QC staff	Set by top management
Role of QC experts	Inspecting out defects	A resource to help workers

There are a number of approaches to the issue of improving quality. Some common elements which they share are:

- To be competitive a company must have a commitment to quality which runs right through the organization. It is not enough for quality to be seen as the responsibility of the quality inspectors or quality control department. This does not just mean that everyone should pay lip service to the idea; it has some quite profound implications. For example, if there is a quality problem, production should be halted till it is solved; suppliers should be chosen on the basis of quality not price; the company would rather not deliver than deliver products where there were doubts about quality.
- High quality should be achieved through systematic investigation, under-standing and process improvement and not through inspection and correction.
- Companies should train all their workers in statistical methods of quality identification and control, give their workers responsibility for quality control and use quality experts as a resource to help workers improve quality levels.

Main theories

The following are some of the most influential schools of thought about how companies should deal with quality:

Total Quality Control

This expression is generally attributed to Armand V. Feigenbaum.[20] He believed that responsibility for quality should be taken away from the quality control department and spread throughout the organization. He stressed the importance of 'getting it right first time' and that an organization's goal should not be an 'acceptable', financially justifiable level of quality, but rather the habit of improvement. While many Western companies were focused on what they believed was the high cost of going beyond a certain quality level, he highlighted what he called 'the cost of quality' – how much it was costing to inspect, rework defects and all the other expenses associated with faulty production.

Zero Defects

The idea of 'Zero Defects' is associated with Philip B. Crosby, author of the book *Quality Is Free*.[21] The first zero defects programme was launched as part of the US Pershing missile project and a zero defects policy was quickly adopted by many Japanese firms. The basic argument was that the use of complex statistical sampling methods accepted that errors were inevitable and that all a company could do was to inspect, to ensure the defect level never exceeded a certain point. Crosby proposed that by aiming at a goal of zero defects, improvement would replace detection. Moreover, like the other quality approaches, zero defects moved responsibility for quality from the specialist quality department, to everyone concerned with designing, procuring materials for, making, handling, selling and distributing a product.

W. Edwards Deming

Deming proposed that management's job is to set up and continuously improve the systems within which people work.[22] But he did not see the management/worker relationship as adversarial. This is because the main way managers can find opportunities for making improvements is through feedback from those who actually do the job. Managers should not simply try setting work standards which will inhibit people's creativity and maintain the status quo. Instead they should train their staff in methods of work analysis and statistical process control, so that the workers themselves become aware of where and how changes should be made.

Joseph M. Juran

Juran emphasized management's responsibility for quality.[23] He proposed that 80 to 85 per cent of all problems at work are a result of the systems that people work under and only 15 to 20 per cent are due to the workers themselves. In such a scenario there is no point just exhorting workers to make greater efforts or trying to bribe them with elaborate bonus schemes, as these only deal with a minor part of the total potential for improvement. Instead management should rank all the main quality problems, identify the 'vital few' which will give the greatest results and set up projects to deal with the key quality issues.

Basic principles of total quality control

Most quality improvement programmes contain some of the following features:

- Quality is seen as the responsibility of the whole organization and top management will clearly be seen to prioritize quality above volume and delivery performance.
- The goal is continuous improvement towards no defects.
- Workers are trained in quality control techniques and given responsibility for inspection. The quality control department act as trainers and expert resources to help operators do their job better.
- Workers are trained in machine maintenance and preventive maintenance. They should be allocated time to check their machines daily.
- Quality should be 'easy to see' – the quality performance of key work stations or production groups should be openly displayed for employees and visitors to look at.
- Management believe that the workers have a contribution to make in improving the firm's performance.

47
Just-in-time production

Just in Time (JIT) is an approach to production adopted by many Japanese firms, which is in a sense the opposite to the way Western firms organize their manufacturing.[24] Firms using JIT have become so aggressively and successfully competitive that JIT has earned the nickname 'Japanese Inspired Terror'. A very simplistic explanation of JIT would be to say that goods are only produced as they are needed. So there are no large stocks of parts and materials throughout the production process. However, this would be misleading, as it classes JIT as being a technique specific to manufacturing, when in fact it is almost a total business philosophy, which affects marketing, quality, productivity, cost, buying and worker motivation.

JIT and continuous improvement

The way that JIT works is usually displayed by a boat on a lake. The water symbolizes all the safety stock and extra time which is built into most production or administrative processes. Underneath the water are rocks which represent all the inefficiencies and problems in most operations. Because there is so much water (safety stock and time) the boat never hits the rocks. However, JIT aims to start reducing the extra time and stock, so that gradually the previously hidden problems come to the surface. Then there is a choice – build more safety stock or time back into the process or else solve the problems. With JIT you solve the problems, reduce safety time further, hit the next problems, solve them, and so on. JIT has been called 'stockless' production. Usually it will never reach that stage, but that is the aim. JIT principles thus lead to a process of continuous improvement rather than an attempt to stabilize a production system with a certain 'acceptable' level of built-in inefficiency.

This puts JIT in sharp contrast to Western production systems like Materials Requirements Planning (MRP) and Optimized Production Technology (OPT). Both of these are based on establishing a stable functioning system. They take for granted that some machine set-ups will take a certain amount of time, that there will always be a carefully calculated level of defects and that particular areas will be bottlenecks. They then construct a system to take account of these factors. The JIT approach is that by constant improvement set-ups can be reduced, quality improved and bottlenecks eliminated.

Japanese JIT ideas have been contrasted with what has been called the Western JIC philosophy (Just in Case), because in the West we build in inefficiencies, just in case something goes wrong:

- In JIT stock is an expensive liability to be reduced to a minimum; in JIC you need safety stocks because of long set-up times, breakdowns, mismatch in the capacities of different areas, changes in customer demand and quality problems.
- In JIT you try to reduce production batch sizes, set-ups and queues at machines; in JIC you calculate economic order quantities based on an acceptance of set-up times, defect levels and queues.
- In JIT you expect to gradually reduce the cost of producing any item; in JIC you try and hold the cost at a certain level.
- In JIT shop-floor workers and supervisors have responsibility for continuous improvement; in JIC experts design and implement the system.

Benefits of JIT

The act of reducing batch sizes to a minimum gives many more benefits to a firm than a simple saving on stock holding costs. Some of the most important are:

- Less stock has to be moved, stored, counted, checked, moved again and so on, so there are lower indirect handling costs.
- Quality problems are detected more quickly, and, as batches are smaller, if a whole batch is affected, fewer items will be wasted. Moreover, as people will be working on goods which have just been produced by a previous work station, it is much easier to trace back and solve any quality problem. In the West materials can wait several weeks between operations, making it extremely difficult to discover why faulty batches occurred.
- Delays, errors, bottlenecks and other problems become much more visible with JIT than when they are hidden by safety stocks and built-in waiting time. This means they can be more easily solved, leading to smoother production and an increase in worker involvement and motivation.
- In JIT operations there tends to be a feeling that people are in control and are actively managing the system. Under Western production systems very often there is a sense of the system being in control (or out of control) and of people being almost unable to affect it.

JIT and marketing

JIT can have a considerable influence on a firm's marketing strategy and competitiveness. Because of the effects of the learning curve, typically a Western company could expect production costs to drop between 5 and 15 per cent for every doubling of volume produced. However, using a JIT continuous improvement approach a Japanese firm could aim at a 20 to 30 per cent reduction in costs for a doubling in volume. This allows the Japanese firm to price lower than its Western competitors, in the knowledge that by generating extra sales, it will substantially contribute to cost reduction and profit margin increase. Western firms who see costs as generally fairly static are unable to compete with the more aggressive Japanese pricing strategies.

Supplier relations

Another area where JIT will have a major effect is on relationships with suppliers. The traditional Western approach to suppliers is to buy at the lowest cost. Also firms tend to 'dual source' or 'multiple source' – have two or more suppliers for many items. This allows them to play one supplier off against another in price-bargaining and it also means that if one supplier lets them down, there is another who can make up any shortages. This way of dealing with suppliers tends to create an adversarial relationship, where suppliers are constantly under threat of being dropped if a buyer receives a cheaper bid from a competitive supplier.

Because JIT is based on buying small quantities frequently to meet current production needs and because there are little or no safety stocks, it normally leads to a relationship in which a supplier is seen as a partner rather than an adversary. With JIT you cannot afford to have late shipments, short orders, or faulty batches, because you do not have the safety stock to keep production running. Therefore, with your suppliers you are looking to find someone who will provide constant, small deliveries of high quality goods. This requires a close working relationship based on trust and mutual help. The table gives some typical differences between traditional (Western) buying behaviour and a JIT model.

Traditional Buying	JIT Buying
Few, large deliveries	Many, small deliveries
Emphasis on price	Emphasis on broader service
Switch to cheaper suppliers	Build long-term relations
Tension in relationship	Supplier seen as partner
Give clear specifications	Involve suppliers and use their expertise in specifying parts

Starting JIT

A company cannot decide to switch to JIT overnight. Changing is a complex process and many Japanese companies have been unsuccessful in their attempts to move to JIT. The only way to start the process is to begin removing those factors which hinder JIT. The sorts of actions a firm could take would be:

- Identify each area where there is safety stock, buffer stock, queues and waiting time. Analyse why these are necessary and take action to deal with these.

- Analyse all set-up times. Do they need to take as long as they do? Could they be performed faster through better training of operators, using more people for the set-up, small adjustments in machines, having tools more easily available and so on? Develop an action plan to reduce set-ups as the less time a set-up takes, the smaller the economic order quantity will be.
- Review the number of suppliers for each item you buy. Choose less important parts and gradually reduce the level of stocks and number of suppliers. Invite suppliers to your plant, explain about your move to JIT and offer them long-term contracts if they can fit in to your need for frequent small deliveries. When this is functioning, extend the process to more important items.
- Start forming problem-solving groups with workers and supervisors, give these time and management support, and do not let so-called 'technical experts' impose their systems but make them resources to the problem-solving groups.

48
Getting the best from people

Konosuke Matsushita, the founder of one of the world's largest corporations, has probably expressed, more clearly than anyone else, a crucial difference between Japanese and Western organizations. In an interview given in 1985 he said:

> We are going to win and the industrial West is going to lose: there is nothing much you can do about it, because the reasons for your failure are within yourselves.
>
> Your firms are built on the Taylor model: even worse, so are your heads. With your bosses doing the thinking, while the workers wield the screwdrivers, you are convinced deep down that this is the right way to run a business.
>
> Only by drawing on the combined brain power of all its employees can a firm face up to the turbulence and constraints of today's environment.
>
> This is why our large companies give their employees three to four times more training than yours, this is why they foster within the firm such intensive exchange and communication; this is why they seek constantly everybody's suggestions . . .

Many Japanese firms have both recognized the contribution which their employees can make, and found ways of making it a reality.

The seven-S framework

One analysis of how Japanese and Western companies differ in how they treat their people has been given in the book *The Art of Japanese Management* by Richard Pascale and Anthony Athos.[26] They identify seven levers which managers can use to influence complex organizations. Three of these, the hard Ss – strategy, structure and systems – are the areas where Western companies have traditionally focused their energy. The four soft Ss – style, skills, staff and super-ordinate goals – have often been neglected by managers in the West. Our corporations have tended to be strongly hierarchical, driven from the top and dedicated to financial performance measures and have treated people lower down as objects, to be acquired and disposed of as circumstances dictated.

Education

There has been a tendency amongst Western media and managers to caricature the Japanese work-force as possibly unthinking servants of the 'Great Corporation'. However, the facts show that Japan has one of the most highly educated work-forces in the world. A comparison of the percentage of people who remain in full-time education until the age of eighteen shows significant differences between Japan and many Western countries:

Country	Percentage of People in Full-Time Education till 18
Japan	94
USA	79
Western Europe	41
France	58
Italy	40
Britain	32

Another study, which looked at the percentage of top managers with degrees in developed countries, also showed the relatively high educational level of the Japanese:

Country	Percentage of Top Managers with University Degrees or Equivalent
Japan	85
USA	85
France	65
West Germany	62
Britain	24

Some Western companies have a tendency to look down on and patronize both their workers and the consumers who buy their products. Much of Western advertising, for example, talks down to people rather than appealing to their intelligence. However, in Japan, with highly educated employees and consumers, companies have to treat them as thinking adults.

Training and skills

In addition to being better educated before they start work, Japanese employees tend to receive significantly more training at work than their Western counterparts. While reliable comparative figures are more difficult to come by, one estimate is that while Japanese, West German and French companies spend 1–2 per cent of their turnover on training, the figure for the USA is around 0.5 per cent or less and for Britain about 0.15 per cent.

This lack of emphasis on people development is reflected in the way many British and American companies invest in automation. In both countries, there is a tendency to accompany automation with the removal of 'costly' skilled workers and their replacement by fewer, 'cheaper' unskilled staff – often part-time female staff. British and American accounting systems help justify this approach, as the cost difference between a number of skilled and a smaller number of unskilled employees can be accurately measured. What the accounting systems do not show is how much production is lost because the unskilled staff do not have the knowledge or motivation to get the best from the equipment. A typical scene from an American or British factory is expensive machinery standing idle until a specialist maintenance mechanic is available because the operators have no mechanical knowledge. In West Germany and Japan, the aim is to keep and develop skilled workers, as firms know that having invested in new facilities, you need the most, rather than the least, qualified people to run them effectively.

Commitment to people

The commitment shown by Japanese companies to their employees can also be seen in other aspects of their operations:

Company goals

The major corporations, and many smaller and medium-sized ones, generally have goals which are both a challenge to employees and which express some concern for employees' welfare; whereas in the West there are still companies who express their aims in terms of providing a certain return to shareholders – a goal which is hardly likely to motivate people on the shop floor.

Long-term employment

As many Japanese employees will spend most of their working lives in one or two companies, they tend to clearly identify their prosperity with that of their employer. This contrasts sharply with the West, where managers, for example, generally see any job as a short-term assignment, forming part of an overall career progression. So while Western managers will often be looking for some quick results to fuel their next career move, Japanese managers realize they will have to live with the results of their actions and so tend to take a more balanced longer-term view of their role in the organization.

Moreover, as companies in Japan realize they cannot hire and fire at will, they tend to take great care with recruitment and make consistent efforts to upgrade the skills of the staff they have. Most vacancies in Japanese firms will be filled by promoting people already inside the organization, so the company sees that it is in its interest to ensure the quality of the available labour force is as high as possible.

Job rotation and interdependency

While people in Western companies tend to specialize in one aspect, such as finance, marketing or production, and move from company to company, in Japan firms often try to give their employees wider experience by moving them to different jobs. One advantage of this practice is that people gain a better understanding of the interdependence of different departments and functions. There is thus less of the functional isolation and fewer of the interdepartmental barriers which are found in Western firms.

Work groups and participation

Great emphasis is placed, in many Japanese companies, on the harmonious functioning of the work group, even to the point of discouraging individualism.

We need to find ways of making work more enjoyable

One of the measures used for judging suitability for promotion is the ability to foster teamwork within an area and between areas. This leads to supervisors and managers seeing their role as coordinators of skilled staff, rather than controllers of recalcitrant workers. Quality circles are one aspect of this as are group-based performance feedback and the designing of jobs to build group, rather than individual, motivation.

Some commentators have explained Japanese firms' attention to their people's needs as being particular to their group-based culture. The suggestion is that such an approach would be less applicable to a society based on individualism, as we in the West. But others have argued that, whatever their culture, people want some form of self-fulfilment, respect, friendship and security from their work. What Japanese companies have been able to do is to go further to meeting these needs than their Western competitors. As a result they have reaped the benefits of greater employee involvement, innovation and commitment.

49
Role of the trade unions

Until the 1950s, wealth in Japan was concentrated in the hands of a few powerful families, and workers tended to live under significantly worse conditions than their counterparts in the West. There were often several unions in most large plants and relations between management and unions were, in general, confrontational, with each side using its power to wring concessions from the other. However, quite quickly in the 1950s, the Japanese moved to a position of single union representation and co-operation with management, with the aim of creating wealth to be shared by both parties. In West Germany and the Scandinavian countries, the West has started to develop in a similar direction to the Japanese. However, in the USA, Britain and some southern European countries, relations between management and unions still show many features of a confrontational rather than cooperative approach.

Unions as images of management

It is easy for some Western managers to view unions as obstructive to change, politically to the left and generally acting against the interests of the company. But this is far too simplistic a view. Unions are 'secondary' organizations – that is, they are dependent for their structure and operating methods on how companies function. They are, in a sense, mirror images of the management with which they deal. If there is a long history of unions being excluded from decision-making, of the company tightly controlling wage costs and replacing skilled full-time workers with cheaper, unskilled part-timers, if new machinery has been introduced over the workers' heads and there has been a clear social gulf between management and the work-force, then the union will develop a culture which is hostile to the company and defensive of the status quo. But if there has been openness from the company and an enlightened approach to labour relations, unions will tend to reflect this in being more constructive towards management. Too often managers fail to see the responsibility they bear for the state of their relations with the trade unions.

Another common mistake management in the West make is to assume that it is better to deal with a weak union than a strong one, and preferable to negotiate with a low-quality union representative rather than one who is astute and well-informed. Agreements made with feeble unions and inadequate negotiators will only turn out to be bad agreements, which will demotivate the work-force, increase the gulf between management and employees, and eventually lead to low productivity and conflict. Agreements forced on weak unions are pyrrhic victories, which usually return to haunt the management who made them.

Wealth creation versus wealth distribution

The central problem behind the state of industrial relations in some of the less successful Western countries appears to be that, whereas the Japanese focus on wealth creation, we in the West have been obsessed with wealth distribution – the division of the spoils. We have therefore not thought through how the wealth we are fighting over can be earned in the first place. The fact that the idea of union representatives on company boards is still an anathema to businessmen and politicians in Britain and America shows how far some countries are from understanding that workers and management do share common interests. In West Germany and Scandinavia workers' representatives have long since been involved in company decision-making.

Currently some company managements are trying to work more closely with unions in the implementation of change. But it is not always clear whether this is due to a genuine understanding of the need to involve unions more closely in the company's activities, or whether management are just taking advantage of the present weakness of unions.

Possible roles for unions

If one was to forget about much of the accumulated bad feeling between management and unions in the West and imagine that both clearly understood it was in their mutual interest to create wealth, then there are several possible roles one could develop for unions:

Leaders of change

If change was clearly in the interest of a company and its work-force, then by having credibility with workers, unions could help managers implement change programmes faster. In West Germany, Scandinavia and Japan new investments may cause workers to be moved to other jobs. However, they do not normally put them out of work. But in Britain and America, where every investment has to be justified by financially measurable payback criteria, savings through loss of jobs are often the only way managers can prove an investment will be viable.

Guardians of 'good management'

Because unions understand that the welfare of their members is dependent on the economic health of the firm, they can act as a kind of quality control on management. If they see that management are taking bad decisions and clearly under-performing, then unions could use their power to influence the company to take action. There has never yet been a strike over a demand that bad management should be replaced – though in many firms there ought to have been.

Industry experts

As unions have access to most companies working in a particular industry, they probably have as much, if not more, information about that industry as management. They could use their position as industry experts to lobby government policy in the interests of their members and to alert managers to any fundamental problems or opportunities in the industry.

Co-directors

Given that unions are interested in safeguarding firms' health to improve the lot of their members, union representatives ought to be an active part of a company's decision-making process. So they ought to be given some places on the board of directors. After all, decisions which are made in full consultation with the unions will have greater legitimacy for workers than policies made unilaterally by management.

Implications for management

If we were to move even a small part of the way towards the kind of cooperative models proposed above, then a number of behavioural changes would be necessary from management. These might include:

- ensuring that union representatives are of a high standard; giving them support to go on short courses in communication, business and negotiation;
- involving union representatives in key management meetings and spending time explaining the background to decisions;
- giving unions annual or twice-yearly presentations of company accounts and of plans for the next six to twelve months;
- starting participative decision-making, with union involvement, right down through the company;
- understanding that workers will normally have divided loyalties between the union and the company then not trying to entice workers away from the union, but rather moving the company's and union's interests more in line with each other so the employees' loyalty to the union naturally reinforces their loyalty to the company;
- seeing that unions often represent particular crafts and skill groups and using the union members' pride in their work to contribute to the quality of the company's products;
- realizing that until unions are integrated into the company's operations, they will tend to adopt an adversarial relationship towards management.

50
Fashions, fads and quick fixes

Many Western industries may have suffered badly at the hands of foreign competitors over the last twenty to thirty years. But one industry at least has experienced rapid and uninterrupted growth. The industry in question is the 'business book' industry. Since the 1950s managers have been bombarded by one best-seller after another – every one of them claiming to provide THE ANSWER which managers have so desperately been looking for. But while managers bought the books and tried out one quick fix after another, the people below smiled and shrugged their shoulders resignedly. Because one by-product of an inconsistent approach to management is the BOHICA Syndrome – when subordinates see a new management toy looming over the horizon they just shake their heads in bemusement at management's fickleness and say 'Bend Over Here It Comes Again'.

Not all the new theories have been bad. In fact, many were based on very sound thinking. But there has been a tendency for them to be picked up, tried for a while and then dropped in favour of the next management fashion. This has often led to managers being distracted from dealing with the deeper problems underlying many Western firms' failure to compete. This would not have been so serious if the management fads had all been fairly consistent in their thinking. But unfortunately the 'experts' seem to perform a 180° about-turn every ten years or so and preach exactly the opposite of what was previously hailed as the WAY FORWARD.

It may be a useful exercise to look back over the last forty years of management thinking and highlight the serious and not so serious contributions the many best-selling authors have made.

The 1950s

The 1950s were a decade when management was viewed as a science. Numbers and structure were the way to run an organization. Theory X was the dominant management style – authoritarian, influenced by Taylorism and work study principles, concerned about production and sales rather than people. Some of the main trends were:

Centralized corporate planning

In the fairly stable political and economic environment of the 1950s the major corporations tended to have large centralized corporate planning departments.

These produced the corporations' long-range plans, which were then handed down to the operating divisions to be carried out.

Management by objectives (MBO)

Possibly the most influential theory in the 1950s of how to manage is generally attributed to Peter Drucker.[29] With MBO executives had their goals set through a process of negotiation with their immediate superior. These goals usually were expressed through quantified targets against which actual performance could be clearly compared.

Diversification

This was seen as the way forward for larger companies. They believed they had 'scientific' management skills which could be applied to any business. So to protect themselves against cycles in demand for their own products, they embarked on a spree of buying up often totally unrelated businesses and then imposed their centralized control on them.

The 1960s

In the 1960s the pendulum seemed to swing in the opposite direction. Reflecting the social changes, people rather than the numbers were now the central issue. Managers were sent away to T-Group sessions to be trained to be sensitive to others – this was the so-called 'touchy-feely' style of management. One influential tool was the Management Grid developed by Robert A. Blake and Jane S. Mouton.[30] This was a matrix used to help classify managers according to their concern for people and concern for results. At the time, the most common finding was that managers were too results-oriented and needed to increase their awareness of people, particularly their understanding of group dynamics and effective team-building.

Theory X – authoritarian management by numbers – was replaced by Theory Y – getting the best from your people through helping them develop and satisfy their self-fulfilment needs. As part of this move away from the numbers towards people issues, firms started to decentralize, to give those lower in the organization greater freedom of action and responsibility. Large, centralized planning staffs were out of fashion – operating divisions were given some (often limited) control over their own destiny.

The 1970s

The key features of the 1970s were the changes in the economic environment in which firms operated. The 1950s and 1960s had been a time of continuous and stable economic growth. But the 1970s saw the major oil crises and subsequent recessions, high levels of inflation in the industrialized countries and the appearance of competition from Japan.

These were seen as turbulent times and long-range centralized corporate planning techniques, where head office knew best, were no longer appropriate.

Instead the move was towards breaking larger companies up into Strategic Business Units (SBUs) in the belief that an SBU could be more aware of and responsive to changes in its environment than a massive corporate HQ could be. The firm was now seen as a portfolio of businesses, each of which had its own strategic plan depending on its position in its particular market. 'Strategic' was probably the main buzz word of the 1970s. To help companies assess the strengths and weaknesses of their collection of SBUs, strategic planning matrices were developed by two major consultancies – the McKinsey Group and the Boston Consulting Group (BCG). The BCG matrix with its classification of SBUs into dogs, stars, cows or question marks is no doubt the most well known. (Some of the crucial weaknesses of these strategic planning matrices are discussed in the chapter on Strategy.) Yet in spite of, and possibly partly because of, these ingenious models the Japanese advance continued almost unopposed.

Another idea which developed in the 1970s was that of Zero Based Budgeting. Now, instead of just taking the previous year's budget and trying to add on a few per cent, executives were being asked to start from zero each year and re-justify every expense in their area of responsibility.

The 1980s

Probably more than any previous decade the 1980s were the time of business fads. 'Excellence' became the goal. We were told to 'stick to the knitting' and offered the 'One Minute Manager'.[31] Although both books became mega best-sellers, history will show whether they ever really made a lasting contribution to the art/science of management. One suspects not.

No doubt the most important influence on business thought during the 1980s was the realization that Japanese companies were clearly doing something a lot better than their reeling Western competitors. Experts and managers dutifully trooped off to Japan to discover the great secret. But when they came back and wrote their books, there was not always full agreement about what should be done. The result was that we were given Quality Circles, Just-In-Time Manufacturing with zero inventory, and Strategic Intent. Theory Z – really making an effort to involve and develop employees – replaced Theory Y, and there were, of course, Corporate Missions, Intrapreneuring, Corporate Culture and the Seven Ss.

Another important feature of the 1980s was the 'funny money' approach to becoming rich. Having realized they could not compete with the Japanese, managers in Britain and America started devising all sorts of brilliant schemes like Management Buy-Outs, Leveraged Buy-Outs, Junk Bonds and so on. By buying and selling companies and, in the process saddling firms with crippling levels of debt repayments, managers and financial wizards emerged wealthy, leaving the companies to pay for their short-sighted avarice.

The 1990s

There's no knowing what the best-sellers of the 1990s will be. Probably one or two will be about getting back to basics and running a company by the numbers.

But most are likely to continue in the employee participation, breaking down barriers, encouraging innovation vein. Maybe.

But one thing is sure – the corporate self-help books market will continue to thrive.

References

1 J. M. Juran, *Quality Control Handbook* (1951); 'Product Quality – A Prescription for the West', *Management Review*, 70 (July 1981); R. Chapman Wood, 'The Prophets of Quality', *The Quality Review* (Winter 1988).
2 R. M. Stogdill, *Handbook of Leadership* (1974); H. J. Eysenck, 'Personality Patterns in Various Groups of Businessmen', *Occupational Psychology*, 41 (1967); I. B. Myers Briggs, *The Myers Briggs Type Indicator* (1962).
3 R. R. Blake and J. S. Mouton, *The Managerial Grid* (1964). See also R. Likert, *New Patterns of Management* (1961); R. Likert, *The Human Organisation* (1963); R. Tannenbaum and W. H. Schmidt, 'How to Choose a Leadership Pattern', *Harvard Business Review*, 51 (1973).
4 F. E. Fiedler, *A Theory of Leadership Effectiveness* (1967); V. H. Vroom and E. L. Deci (eds), *Management and Motivation* (1970); J. Adair, *Effective Leadership* (1983).
5 R. M. Belbin, *Management Teams: Why They Succeed or Fail* (1981).
6 I. L. Janis, *Victims of Group-Think* (1972).
7 J. Child, *Organisation: A Guide to Problems and Practice* (1984).
8 R. Harrison, 'How to Describe Your Organization', *Harvard Business Review* (Sept–Oct 1972).
9 A. Pettigrew, *The Awakening Giant: Continuity and Change in I.C.I.* (1985).
10 M. E. Porter, *Competitive Advantage* (1985).
11 Studies carried out for the White House Office of Consumer Affairs. The results are summarized in K. Albrecht and R. Zemke, *Service America!* (1985).
12 T. Buzan, *Use Your Head* (1974).
13 Source: W. Dean, Japanese Business Policy Unit, Warwick Business School.
14 P. Doyle, J. Saunders and V. Wong, 'Japanese Marketing Strategies in the UK: A Comparative Study', *Journal of International Business Studies* (Spring 1986).
15 P. Doyle, *What Happened to Britain's Economic Miracle?* (1988).
16 'UK Management Training and Development – Too Little, Too Late, For Too Few', IR-RR (May 1987) and *The Making of Managers. A Report on Management Education, Training and Development in the United States, West Germany, France, Japan and the UK*, NEDC Books.
17 Source: M. Cooley, author of *Architect or Bee*.
18 M. E. Porter, *Competitive Advantage* (1985).
19 R. Wild, *Production and Operations Management* (1984).

20 R. Chapman Wood, 'The Prophets of Quality', *The Quality Review* (Winter 1988); A. V. Feigenbaum, *Total Quality Control* (3rd edn, 1983).
21 P. B. Crosby, *Quality is Free* (1979).
22 M. Tribus, *Deming's Way*, Process Management Institute Inc.
23 J. M. Juran, *Quality Control Handbook* (1951).
24 For a clear presentation of JIT ideas see R. J. Schonberger, *Japanese Manufacturing Techniques* (1982).
25 'Why the West Will Lose: Extracts from Remarks Made by Mr Konosuke Matsushita to a Group of Western Managers', *Industrial Participation* (Spring 1985).
26 R. T. Pascale and G. Athos, *The Art of Japanese Management* (1981).
27 R. Johnson, 'Youth Training in Europe', *Personnel Management* (July 1984); R. Johnson, 'Adult Training in Europe', *Personnel Management* (August 1984).
28 See note 16.
29 P. F. Drucker, *The Practice of Management* (1955).
30 See note 3.
31 T. J. Peters and R. H. Waterman, *In Search of Excellence* (1982); K. Blanchard and S. Johnson, *The One Minute Manager* (1982).

Index

accountancy gap *183–4*
adhocracy *54–5*
administration and turnaround *117*
'adolescence' of group *30*
adult ego state *24–6*
advantage, differential *124–6*
agenda of meetings *39*
agents of change *76*
agreement *73*
analytical thinking *154–5*
assigning activities in meetings *41*
associative thinking *166–7*
assumptions *157*
Athos, A. *197*
audit, organization *130*
awareness as source of power *59–60*

bad times and good times *78–81*
balance in meetings *40*
barriers to creative thinking *156–7*
basics, returning to *109*
BCG *see* Boston Consulting Group
behaviour
    consumer, and marketing *132–5*
    counter-cultural *76*
    group *31–2, 33*
    and management style *11*
    and organizations *45*
Belbin, R. M. *32*
benefits of meetings *42*
Berne, E. *23*
'birth' of group *29*
Blake, R. A. *206*
blueprinting *149*
Boston Consulting Group matrix *89–92, 207*
brainstorming *158–61, 162–3*
brand leader *130–1*
build strategy *90, 91*
bureaucracy *53–4*
buying
    and marketing *144–5, 146*
    process, model of *132–3*
    types of purchase *133*
    see also customers
Buzan, T. *166*

'cash cows' *89, 90, 91, 96*
centralized planning *205–6*
'chairman', group *33*
change
    managing process *74–7*
    organizational structure *48–51*
    and political activity *57*
    problem sensing *68–9*
    and resistance *64–7*
    responses to need for *78–81*
    starting process *70–3*
    unions as leaders of *203*
child ego state *24–6*
'childhood' of group *29–30*
choice
    of management style *14, 72–3*
    of solution *164*
    of strategy *86*
    of transition manager *71–2*
classical organizational structure *44–5*
client and problem-solving meeting *162*
co-directors *204*
coercion and change *73*
committees *see* groups
common interest identified *19–20*
communication *73, 125*
'company worker', group *33*
competition
    competitor targets *128–9*
    perfect *124*
    and time *85–6*
complaints *135*
complementary transactions *25*
compliance and change *69*
concern and change *68*
conflict resolver, manager as *7–8*
conformity in group *35–6, 37*
conservatism, dynamic *57, 79*
consistency *48–9*
consumers *see* customers
content of change *64–5*
contingency theory *11–12, 45–6*
continuous learning strategy *110*
contract, informal *5*

control   *44, 130*
coordinator, manager as   *8*
copying services   *148–9*
corporation *see* organizations
cost
    cutting and decline   *114*
    and price   *136, 137*
counter-cultural behaviour   *76*
'creative destruction'   *141*
creativity
    brainstorming   *158–61*
    mind-mapping   *166–9*
    problem-solving   *162–5*
    quality circles   *170–3*
    thinking   *154–7, 174–6*
crisis and change   *69, 80*
Crosby, P. B.   *189, 191*
crossed transactions   *25*
culture, organizational   *52–5, 207*
customers/consumers
    behaviour   *132–5*
    buyer power   *99*
    dissatisfied   *135*
    economic value to   *145*
    motivation   *133–4*
    needs   *140–1*
    orientation   *110*
    satisfaction   *186–8*
    serving   *109*
    targets, choosing   *128*
    see also buying

DA *see* differential advantage
decision-making unit   *134–5, 145*
decline   *113–17, 143*
defence mechanisms and change   *80–1*
delegation in meetings   *41*
demand and pricing   *138*
Deming, W. E.   *189, 191*
democracy   *55*
detail hunting   *80*
'deviants'   *76–7*
differential advantage   *124–6*
differentiation   *46–7*
discounting change   *79*
discrimination, price   *137*
dissatisfied customers   *135*
diversification   *206*
DMU *see* decision-making unit
'dogs'   *89, 90, 91, 97*
doomsday scenario   *69*
downstream links   *105–6*
Drucker, P.   *206*
dynamic conservatism   *57, 79*

economic value to customer   *145*
economic/rational people   *12–13*
education and training   *73*
    and creative thinking   *155–6*
    Japan   *198–9*

effective meetings   *39–42*
ego states   *23–5*
elasticity, demand   *138*
emergent behaviour in groups   *31–2*
emotional reactions to change   *65, 80*
employees/subordinates   *12, 111*
    see also participation
ending meeting   *41–2*
enrichment, job   *16–17*
environment, of organizations   *12, 14*
evaluation, brainstorming   *160–1*
'evaluator', group   *33*
EVC *see* economic value to customer
evolutionary strategy   *101*
executive defence mechanisms   *80–1*
executive summary   *151*
existing markets   *122*
experience and pricing   *137–8*
expertise as source of power   *60*
experts, industry   *204*

facilitator, manager as   *7*
fashions and fads   *205–8*
feedback   *164*
Feigenbaum, A. V.   *189, 191*
'financial' strategy versus 'market
    share'   *182–5*
'finisher', group   *34*
focus, strategic   *127–8*
follow-up to meetings   *42*
force-field analysis   *74–5*
formal groups   *28–30*
'forming', group   *29*
freezing and change   *68*
fulfilment *see* self-actualization

General Electric matrix   *93–4*
geographic analysis   *94*
goals *see* objectives
good times and bad times   *78–81*
government, in Japan   *180*
groups
    behaviour and roles   *31–4*
    brainstorming   *158–61, 162–3*
    formation   *28–30*
    groupthink   *37*
    meetings   *39–42, 162–4*
    mind-mapping   *168–9*
    negative aspects   *32–8*
    problem-solving   *163–4*
    team worker   *34*
    work   *18, 200–1*
growth and product life cycle   *142*

Harrison, R.   *52*
harvest strategy   *91*
headlining   *41, 176*
helping   *73*
'heretics'   *76–7*
Herzberg, F.   *17–18*

hierarchy of needs   2–3, 18
hold strategy   91
human resources and decline   114

ideas
    evaluation   160–1
    generation   164
    see also creativity
identification
    and change   69
    of common interest   19–20
    of value   103
ignoring change   79
images of management, unions as   202–3
implementation
    of brainstorming   161
    of change   75–7
    of marketing strategy   130
    of quality circles   172–3
implications of portfolio analysis   91–2
implicit coercion and change   73
improvement, continuous   193–4
industrial marketing   144–6
industry structure analysis   98–101
informal contract   5
informal groups   28
informal meetings   42
information
    distribution   39
    lack of   36
    as source of power   61–2
innovation   17, 64, 109
intangibility of services   147
integration   29–30, 47
interaction matrix and strategy   86–7
internalization and change   69
intrapreneuring   207
introduction of new technology   17
involvement see participation
invulnerability and group   37

Janis, I.   37
Japan   97
    customer satisfaction   186–8
    just-in-time   193–6
    marketing   127, 129–30, 134
    people   197–201
    quality important   170–3, 189–92
    strategy   107, 111–12, 182–5
    trade unions   202–4
JIT see just-in-time
job
    enrichment   16–17
    long-term, in Japan   199–200
Juran, J. M.   189, 191–2
just-in-time production   193–6, 207

latent markets   122
laziness   157
leaders

of change, unions as   203
of problem-solving meeting   162–3
learning
    curve and pricing   137–8
    strategy, continuous   110
left-brained approach   123
life cycle, product   95, 128
    and marketing   140–3
linear thinking   166–7
linkages   104–6
Little (Arthur D.)   95
long-term actions   117
long-term approach to strategy   180
long-term employment in Japan   199–200

McKinsey and Co.   93
maintenance behaviour in groups   32
Management Grid   206
management, pro-active see change;
    creativity; fashions; groups; Japan;
    marketing; organizations; people; roles;
    strategy
manipulation   73
    political   37–8
    strategy   101
mapping see mind-mapping
market
    current situation   151
    growth and position   89–92
    penetration   136
    research   187–8
    share strategy   184–5
marketing   121
    concept   120–3
    differential advantage   124–6
    industrial   144–6
    and just-in-time   194–5
    plan, writing   150–2
    and product life cycle   140–3
    services   147–9
    setting prices   136–9
    strategy development   127–31
    and turnaround   117
    see also customers
Maslow, A.   2–3, 18
matrix approach see portfolio analysis
Matsushita, K.   197
'maturity' of group   30
    and product life cycle   142–3
MBO (management by objectives)   206
medium-term actions   116–17
meetings see under groups
memory and mind maps   168
message of need for change   75
mind-mapping   166–9
mindset   157
minutes   41, 164
mistakes, pricing   138
mix, marketing, developing   129–30
'monitor', group   33

monopoly   124
motivation   2–5
   customer   133–4
   strategy   110
Mouton, J. S.   206
moving and change   68

needs
   of customers   140–1
   hierarchy of   2–3, 18
   of subordinates   12
negative aspects
   of groups   35–8
   of meetings   41
negative attitudes to change   61
negative source of power   61
negotiation   19–22, 73
new entrants   99–100
new technology   17, 64
NIH see 'Not Invented Here'
non-product marketing   122–3
'norming', group   30
norms as source of power   60
'Not Invented Here' syndrome   157

objectives
   of change process   75
   of Japanese management   179–80, 199
   management by   206
   of marketing plan   152
   of meetings   39
   strategic   127
obstacles, return to   175
open coercion and change   73
opportunities in SWOT analysis   84–7
options, marketing   151–2
organizations
   audit   130
   corporate missions   207
   culture   52–5, 207
   decline   113–17
   environment   12, 14, 85
   Japanese corporation   181
   and management style   11, 12, 14
   as political systems   56–8
   power in   59–62
   structure   44–7
      changing   48–51
   style   11
   supply chain analysis   105
   SWOT analysis   84–5
orientation, marketing   121–2
ownership in group   36

parent ego state   23–4, 25–6
participation   15–18
   and change   73
   in Japan   200–1
   in meetings   39
   and strategy   111

Pascale, R.   197
patterns   156–7
people, managing
   changing   77
   getting best from   197–201
   involvement, increased   15–18
   motivation   2–5
   negotiation   19–22
   role of manager   6–9
   style of management   10–14
   Transactional Analysis   23–6
perfect competition and monopoly   124
'perfect world' scenario   174–5
'performing', group   30
person culture   55
personality   11, 61
Petronius, Gaius   48
phrasing, positive   175–6
physiological needs   2
planning
   centralized corporate   205–6
   change   71
   marketing plan   150–2
   meetings   39–40
'plant', group   33
PLC see life cycle, product
policy change   75–6
politics/political
   activity and change   57
   and decline   114
   manipulation in group   37–8
   resistance to change   65–6
   support and change   81
   systems, organizations as   56–8
Porter, M. E.   98
portfolio analysis   93–7
   BCG matrix   88–92
portfolios   77
position as source of power   60
positioning   141
positive attitudes to change   66–7
positive phrasing   175–6
power
   culture   52–3
   and industry structure   99
   in organizations   59–62
pragmatic strategy   100–1
price setting and marketing   136–9
primary activities   102–3, 104
problems
   and brainstorming   159–60
   sensing and change   68–9
   shelving in meetings   41
   -solving   162–5
   see also creativity
processes
   of change   64–5
      managing   74–7
      starting   70–3
   management   133

as source of power   60
product   121
    marketing   147–9
    offering, deciding   129
    see also life cycle
production   121
    just-in-time   193–6
    and turnaround   117
profit and loss statement   152
programme, marketing   152
proposals in meetings   40
pull versus push marketing   132
purchasing see buying
push versus pull marketing   132

quality
    circles   18, 170–3, 207
    importance of   189–92
    of services variable   148
'question marks'   89, 90, 91, 97

rational resistance to change   65
rational/economic people   12–13
recipes   156–7
rejection of change   80
reorganization, example   49–50
repertoires   156–7
repositioning   125–6
reputation   3
required behaviour in groups   31–2
resistance and change   64–7
resource/s
    of problem-solving meeting   163
    and reward as source of power   60
'resource investigator', group   33
responses to need for change   78–81
results, quality circles   171–2
reward   60, 76
'ridiculous idea' scenario   174–5
right-brained approach   123
rivalry and industry structure   98–9
roles
    culture   53–4
    of government in Japan   180
    in groups   32–4
    of manager   6–9
    marketing plan   150
    models   76
    of trade unions   202–4

safety/security needs   2
satisfaction, customer   186–8
satisficing   37, 157
SBUs (Strategic Business Units)   45, 207
scapegoat and change   81
self-actualization   3, 12–13
self-esteem   3
self-image   4
self-interest   62
selling see marketing

sensing problem and change   68–9
services, marketing   147–9
Seven-S framework   197, 207
'shaper', group   33
short-term actions   116
skimming, market   136–7
social, people seen as   2, 12–13
solution choice   164
sources of power   59–62
stability of management   111
'stars'   89, 90, 96
stereotyping and group   37
storage of services impossible   147–8
'storming', group   29–30
strategy
    definition of   107–12
    differential advantage basis   125
    'financial' versus 'market share'   182–5
    industry structure analysis   98–101
    Japan   107, 111–12, 180 , 182–5
    managing turnaround   113–17
    marketing   127–31, 151
    pricing   136–8
    Strategic Business Units   45, 207
    supply chain analysis   102–6
    SWOT analysis   84–7
    see also portfolio analysis
strengths
    of person culture   55
    of portfolio analysis   92
    of power culture   53
    of problem-solving group   164–5
    of role culture   53–4
    in SWOT analysis   84–7
    of task culture   54
stretch, organizational   110
structure
    and decline   114
    of marketing plan   151–2
    of organizations   44–7
        changing   48–51
    of quality circles   171
    see also industry structure
style, management   10–14
    choice and change   72–3
subconscious, relying on   175
subordinates see employees
substitutes   100
success   41, 74
suppliers
    linkages   105
    power   99
    relations   195
supply chain analysis   102–6
support   73
    activities   102–3, 104
surprises, avoiding   41
survival
    group   38
    and pricing   137

SWOT analysis   *84–7, 151*
synergies   *110*

TA *see* Transactional Analysis
tactics in meetings   *40*
tasks
    behaviour in groups   *32*
    culture   *54–5*
    during decline   *115–16*
    and management style   *11–12*
Taylor, F.   *15*
'team worker', group   *34*
teams *see* groups
technology, new   *17, 64*
temporary bad times   *79–80*
T-Groups   *206*
thinking, creative   *154–7, 174–6*
threats in SWOT analysis   *84–7*
time and competition   *85–6*
top management and decline   *114, 115*
total quality control   *190, 191, 192*
trade unions   *169, 202–4*
traditions as source of power   *60*
training *see* education and training
trait studies   *10*
Transactional Analysis   *23–6*
transition manager, choice of   *71–2*
trust versus control   *44*
Tuckman's integrative model   *29–30*
turnaround, managing   *113–17*
two-factor theory   *17–18*

uncertainty reduction   *62*
unfreezing and change   *68*

unification strategy   *110*
unions *see* trade unions

value identification   *103*
valuing whole person   *16*
variable quality of services   *148*

weaknesses
    of person culture   *55*
    of portfolio analysis   *95–6*
    of power culture   *53*
    of problem-solving group   *164*
    of role culture   *54*
    in SWOT analysis   *84–7*
    of task culture   *54–5*
wealth creation   *181, 203*
Western countries   *97*
    change resisted   *64–5*
    compared with Japan *see* Japan
    marketing   *120, 123, 126, 140, 144–5*
    strategy   *107–8, 182–3*
    structure   *101*
whole person, valuing   *16*
winning strategy   *111*
withdraw strategy   *91*
work groups   *18, 200–1*

X and Y, Theories   *13, 206, 207*

Z, Theory   *207*
Zero Based Budgeting   *207*
zero defects   *190, 191*